Speak Lord; I Hear

George A. Maloney, S.J.

LIVING FLAME PRESS

325 RABRO DRIVE, HAUPPAUGE, N.Y. 11788

First Printing 1988

Cover By Irene Lang

Copyright© 1988 George A. Maloney, S.J.
Printed in the United States of America

Imprimi Potest: Patrick J. Burns, S.J., Provincial, Wisconsin
Province of the Society of Jesus, May 20, 1987

ISBN: 0-914544-69-1

Published by:
Living Flame Press/325 Rabro Drive/Hauppauge, N.Y. 11788

Printed at Mark IV Press, Hauppauge, N.Y.

Scripture verses from The Jerusalem Bible
Copyright© 1966 by Darton, Longman & Todd, Ltd. and Doubleday & Company, Inc.

Dedication

To Josie Murphy
who teaches children how to listen
to the same Lord she listens to.

Acknowledgement

Sincere thanks to
Mrs. Patricia Metta for typing the manuscript
and to
Sister Joseph Agnes, S.C.H. and
Mrs. June Culver
for careful reading and correcting
of the manuscript
and for other suggestions
that proved most helpful.

TABLE OF CONTENTS

INTRODUCTION

I recently picked up while going through some of my music records the album of Bob Dylan, called *John Wesley Harding*, issued in the latter '60s. I was fascinated by Dylan's modern parable written on the cover of the album. Dylan describes three kings who visit a man named Frank. The first king explains their mission to Frank. "Mr. Dylan has come out with a new record. This record of course features none but his own songs and we understand that you're the key." "That's right," said Frank, "I am."

"Well, then" said the king in a bit of excitement, "could you please open it up for us?" Frank, who all this time had been reclining with his eyes closed, suddenly opened both of them up as wide as a tiger. "And just how far would you like to go in?" he asked. The chief of the kings replies: "Not too far, but just enough so we can say that we've been there."

Today there is a growing hunger among small groups found in all the various Christian Churches for deeper prayer. Like the small "remnant" among the people of God in the Old Testament desert, the *Anawim*, the number of such "desert pilgrims" among Christians today is small. They have heard the question, not from Frank, but from Jesus Christ: "And just how far into the desert would you like to go?" The majority of modern Christians continue to answer: "Not too far, but just enough so we can say that we've been there."

Yet the few, hungry Christians, eager to sell all to obtain the *pearl* of great price, desire to hear their desert guide, Jesus Christ, speak to them and in His outpoured Holy Spirit, they wish to discern how best to follow His guidance.

1

This book has been written for these few who seek greater experience of God as community of love and therefore, are eager to learn how to discern properly the guidance of God's Holy Spirit. It seeks to bring together various aspects of deeper prayer along with teachings on discernment. For without proper discernment, prayer as communication and communion with the Divine Trinity becomes only illusory and dehumanizing.

One of the essential elements of our spiritual life is the ability to discern which movements of our "spirit" are from God's Spirit and which come from "ungodly" spirits. In the Old Testament there were true and false prophets. In the New Testament there were dissensions and various opposing teachers and practices. Throughout Christianity seers and visionaries have appeared with messages from God or the Blessed Virgin, only to be proved to be hysterics.

The Catholic Church, therefore, has been cautious in discerning the proper Spirit of God operating in religious experiences from false "angels" appearing as light. It has developed over 2,000 years of experience a large body of solid, prudent teachers who through their writings give us ways to *discern* the movements of various "spirits" in order that we may always be guided in prudence and discretion by God's Spirit and not by any opposing or contradictory spirits.

I pray these ten chapters may provide instruction and encouragement for you on deeper prayer and the very important area of guidance in your discernment of the true movements of God's Holy Spirit. How far would you like to enter into the desert and there hear the Spirit guiding you to greater loving oneness with the indwelling Trinity and with your neighbor? Give God glory if this book may be of some help to you in answering that question.

Easter, 1987   George A. Maloney, S.J.
St. Patrick's Novitiate
Midway City, CA

Chapter One:

DISCERNMENT OF SPIRITS

One of the essential elements of our spiritual life is the ability to discern which movements of our "spirit" are from God's Spirit and which come from "ungodly" spirits. In the Old Testament there were true and false prophets. In the New Testament there were dissensions and various opposing teachers and practices. Throughout Christianity seers and visionaries have appeared with messages from God or the Blessed Virgin, only to be proved to be hysterics.

The Catholic Church, therefore, has been cautious of private revelations from people who claim, "God told me to tell you. . ." It has developed—over 2,000 years of experience in discernment—a large body of solid, prudent teachers who through their writings give us ways to *discern* the movements of various "spirits" in order that we may always be guided in prudence and discretion by God's Spirit and not by any opposing or contradictory spirits.

St. Ignatius, founder of the Society of Jesus (the *Jesuits*), has given us in his writings, especially in his *Spiritual Exercises*, time-tested methods of finding God's will in life's major choices, but also criteria for sifting out in prayer-experiences what are really right movements from the Holy Spirit.

But such a habit of discernment of the working of God in our lives is an on-going process that is simple, but not always easy. If God has created us to love Him and to experience His undying love for us in Jesus Christ through His Spirit, He must be active so that we might discover His loving "will" operating in our lives and we might cooperate in "doing" His holy will in all things. "Wherefore be not unwise but understanding what the will of the Lord is . . . be filled with the Spirit" (Eph 5:17-18).

Thy Will Be Done

The secret of a happy and successful Christian life is to do each thought, word and deed out of love for God. It is to seek always as Jesus Christ did in His earthly life to please His heavenly Father in all things. Love is provided by deeds, but not just any deeds. The deeds that please God are deeds accomplished according to His holy will. The deeds are important as signs of our total submission in love to please Him. If we love another, we must want to please that person in all things best for that person. Jesus tells us, "If you keep my commandments, you shall abide in my love. Even as I have kept my Father's commandments and abide in his love" (Jn 15:10).

But what does "doing the will" of God mean? In His earthly life Jesus strove always to keep the commandments of the Heavenly Father. ". . . not my will, but thine be done" (Lk 22:42). It is evident that many areas of His life were seen clearly by Him as commands of the Father. Though it cost Him personally whatever price, even His own life, He obeyed what He saw as the clear manifestation of the will of His Father in the commands given Him to fulfill. Surely His agony in the Garden and His death on the cross show us that Jesus regarded dying on the cross for the sins of the world as a clear command of the Father. We know that the basic ten commandments are clear indications of God's will for our conduct in relation to Him and to our neighbors.

4

Memo

Also in His life there were whole areas of decisions that seem to have been made very spontaneously, sometimes with reflection, sometimes in deep, silent prayer. Here we see a more delicate discernment of the will of His loving Father. This goes beyond the mere clear commands of the Father. In all things, in each moment, Jesus seeks to do the slightest *wish* of the Father. This requires greater love, delicacy and discernment to ask what is the wish of the Father in this or that circumstance than merely to do the major commands.

Lastly, there are areas in the Gospel stories wherein a still higher degree of return of love for love is indicated. Jesus wishes to go beyond the command and the wish of the Father in order to "improvise" spontaneous, creative moments to "flesh" out in human terms His return of love for the infinite love He had experienced from the Father toward Him. As the Father's love is an outpouring of total self-giving to His Son, the return of Jesus' love to the Father partakes of a *kenosis*, a self-emptying through "creative suffering."

We will wish to discern the workings of God's Spirit in our lives on various levels of generosity and experienced love. We must believe as Christians that God has a universal will to "save" all of His created children. He wishes all of us to live in harmony with our human nature. How to do this is discovered by the use of our right reason, divine revelation and the teachings of the God-given authority in the Church.

To seek to do God's will, we must believe, therefore, that God has a will for us in our decisions. We must believe that His Spirit will be given to us so we might discover what His will is (Eph 5:17-18). We must also desire not only affectively but also effectively to know that will and be resolved to carry it out. Such choices and decisions should always conform to God's universal will and promote our return of love to God so as never to be self-seeking.

Evaluating Spiritual Experiences

Before we look at discernment of spirits in our major choices or decisions that will determine a radical change in the way we choose to serve in God's kingdom, let us look at various criteria for evaluating the differences in moods, feelings, attractions and our way of discerning which psychosomatic manifestations are truly from the Spirit of God.

The first step in discernment is to be able sensitively to see differences in interior movements on the psychic and spiritual levels that take place in prayer. The disciplines of journaling and the evening examen are helps in getting in touch with such "feelings." In his *Autobiography*, St. Ignatius of Loyola describes his first experience in discernment of spirits. He was being drawn by God away from his worldly life as a gallant soldier to move toward a possible life of total dedication to God's service. He still dreamed of knightly adventures by which he would win the hand of a beautiful lady. Such thoughts made him happy and enthusiastic. When they faded, he fell into feelings of discontent.

When he read the lives of the saints and dreamed of doing great exploits for God he also felt happy and enthusiastic. This happiness, however, persisted. He writes, "After some time his eyes were opened a little, and he began to marvel at the differences and to reflect upon it, realizing from experience that some thoughts left him sad and others happy."

Ignatius had taken the first step in a lifetime of discernment of spirits. We need also a criterion to discern authentic experiences of God in prayer from those that come from other sources. We should know by now that not all experiences of "tingling joy," tranquil peace and even tears, visions, voices, the smell of "celestial" odors, and out-of-the-body experiences are always from God.

Mystical Guidelines

The teachers of true Christian mysticism have always insisted on caution and discernment in judging the source of any mystical experiences. Their first and constant insistence is that visions, voices, levitation, odors and sweet tastes in the mouth with gentle touches by angelic messengers are never to be sought for in prayer. Such balanced teachers were quite unanimous in stressing humility and compunction as the true touchstones of a religious experience with no attention given to the physico-psychic effects. They knew, as they opened up their psyche through altered states of consciousness in deeper prayer, that there could be subjective deviations in judgment, memory and attention. Voices often could be distinctly heard. Visions of the saints, of Jesus Christ, of their beloved deceased could occur. They were very wary that such phenomena never be construed as a sign of sanctity or even the measure of progress in prayer.

The words of St. John of the Cross must be ever kept in mind in dealing with such matter:

> It must be known that even though these apprehensions come to the bodily senses from God, one must never rely on them or accept them. A man should rather flee from them completely, and have no desire to determine whether they be good or bad. The more exterior and corporal they are, the less certain is their divine origin. God's communication is more commonly and appropriately given to the spirit, in which there is greater security and profit for the soul, than to the senses where ordinarily there is extreme danger and room for deception. . . He who esteems these apprehensions is in serious error and extreme danger of being deceived. Or at least he will hinder his spiritual growth, because, as we mentioned, these corporal perceptions bear no proportion to what is spiritual.

Is Peace Always From God?

Another criterion of deeper prayer must be used to determine whether the sense of peace and oneness with God really comes from ourselves or other sources or, indeed, from the Holy Spirit. In deeper prayer, as we yield more of our own doing to the will of the Holy Spirit, we must be on our guard that we do not render ourselves vacuously empty. There is a true emptying of our own power to know God through our own efforts. But there is a higher inner activity that absorbs us. It is an active receptivity that now commands our attention. It is a loving waiting in faith, hope and love on the indwelling Trinity. It is a stretching forth in deeper, more humble self-surrender to God.

God is the center of all our strivings, never ourselves. At times a false peace can cover over areas of our lives that need to be reckoned with in the presence of God for healing before we can go on to a deeper union with God. By focusing on how peaceful we are in moments of prayer rather than in being open to God's workings through the Holy Spirit, we can only delay future progress in the spiritual life.

The ultimate criterion of whether the Holy Spirit is operating in our lives is the sincerity that we encounter in our lives and in our surrendering of our lives to His dominance. This sincerity can be measured not by words alone but by deeds. If we see a godly life lived by a person who claims that God is being experienced in deep prayer, we can recognize that the Spirit of Jesus has met that person deeply and has transformed that life by grace from God and by human cooperation. We should always be suspect of the "mystic" who cares little to serve his/her immediate neighbor or who refuses to listen to any voice other than his/her own inner one. True mystical union with the loving community of the Trinity sends the mystic forward to serve others in listening obedience to God's Word in Scripture, in the magisterium of the Church and in the lives of others.

The Fruit of the Holy Spirit

Another criterion for deciding whether we are truly meeting God in spiritual experiences is found in the traditional teaching of St. Paul who applies the saying of Jesus, "You will know them by their fruits," (Mt 7:20), to discern the working of the Holy Spirit. "But the fruit of spiritual ideals is love, joy, peace, long-suffering, affability, goodness, fidelity, gentleness, self-control. Against such there is no law. . . If we live by spiritual ideals, let us conduct ourselves by these ideals" (Ga 5:22-26).

But it is not always very easy to measure the fruit produced to discern whether the Holy Spirit is truly operating in one's life. Each fruit given by St. Paul can be mistaken for other reactions that neither indicate the action of the Spirit nor flow out of love. How often seeming patience can be a cloak for apathy, affability for crowd acceptance, long-suffering for cowardliness.

We must be aware of the principle in the spiritual life that the signs of the fruit of the Spirit usually appear as a unified growth. Their growth is one of greater unity of personhood in self-giving love and bringing about a progressive increase in basic well-being, joy, peace and consolation.

What To Do?

Let us now turn to the other important aspect of discernment, namely, a method whereby we can discover God's loving will drawing us to make a choice of major importance. I rely on the well-known method of St. Ignatius as outlined in the *Spiritual Exercises* on his rules of discernment in time of an "election." There surely are other methods that are equally as useful.

All of us have faced and will perhaps face major decisions in our lives. We become very confused as we don't know which way to turn, what choice to make. Perhaps two choices confront you. A young widow wonders whether she should marry or remain single. A priest or nun after years of one form of apostolate may be confronted with a change of activity, to switch from teaching to a more direct pastoral ministry or to volunteer to work among the poor in a foreign land.

Any process of discernment presupposes a desire to find peace by resolving the possibilities facing a person. To seek God's help is, as we already said, to believe He has a plan for us, an "alluring," drawing us toward one choice of action over another or others as possibilities. To use such a method to discover God's will requires also a deep and personal relation with Jesus Christ, especially a desire to serve Him in a return of generous self-giving in poverty and humility, in a word, in the creative suffering of the "cross."

Ways of Making a Decision

1. St. Ignatius gives as the first and clearest way to arrive at a decision the case when God dramatically enters into our lives and we are deeply "pushed" in one certain direction, as St. Paul experienced Christ's powerful intervention in his conversion on the way to Damascus (Ac 22:6-16).
2. The second way consists in a less dramatic divine intervention, yet one which brings about a deep sense of peace or rightness about a decision that does not have present other "competing" possibilities. In such a case a spiritual director can be of assistance to assure you and give you trust about what has been so clear without a lengthy process of discernment.
3. The third and usual method for discerning the "best" choice according to God's attractions takes place when you find yourself very confused and disturbed as to what choice to make since there are *pro* and *con* arguments for and against two or more choices.

To Reach a State of Detachment

Ignatius gives us three exercises to give us a larger perspective of vision for the most adequate choice. 1) Imagine yourself on your deathbed and see what choice you would have wished to have made. 2) Picture yourself before the judgment seat of God. How would you like to have decided "back there?" 3) Imagine yourself helping someone else to

10

come to a decision similar to yours. What advice would you give?

A More Rational Approach

When the choice is very complex and time is available for further prayer, you can take the following steps, preferably under a spiritual director.

1. Gather all necessary information that would help you in your choice. This may involve taking a personality and aptitude test, dialoging with your intimate friends, seeking information from experts in a field about which you are relatively uninformed but which would touch your choice.
2. Consider the *cons* or the negative factors, writing them down in a first column.
3. Write down the *pros* or positive elements of your choice in a parallel column.
4. Review prayerfully first the negative list; then the positive one. Then in prayer compare the two. Record how you feel "living" with your tentative choice.
5. Finally make a decision clearly and in well-defined terms of action to be taken to implement the choice made.
6. A word on "peace" that may or may not come with your decision. If you feel not only a lack of peace but doubt, step back and choose the alternative. Live with that choice and check your "feelings."
7. If there is no peace with either choice, postpone your decision if it is possible. If you are pressed to come to a decision, prayerfully make a choice and stay with it. There perhaps is no clear answer and one choice is perhaps as good as the other. You have done all you could and God will bless your choice.

Above all, in all methods of discernment, profess at all times God's goodness, love, guidance and protection of you. If you ask to know God's will, He will surely speak and grant you assurance in faith, hope and love as to what will most please the heavenly Father.

11

Chapter Two:

DISCOVERING THE INDWELLING TRINITY

You and I are in a constant process of becoming our true and unique persons in and through God's trinitarian love. Since our incorporation into the Body of Christ through our Baptism, the fullness of God's personalized love as self-emptying Father, Son and Holy Spirit, resides within us. God, as a community of three divine Persons, cannot give us a greater share of Himself as one divine nature in three distinct but inseparable Persons than by the gift with which He is at this moment gifting us.

The secret of our continued growth in prayer and the Christian spiritual journey is one of growing in greater and greater degrees of awareness and conscious experience of God's immanent or indwelling presence as self-emptying love within us. How absolutely sad that Jesus Christ, God's living Word made flesh, and still revealing to us the mysteries of God through the gift of His Holy Spirit, wishes to lead us into the presence of the Holy Trinity as the Source and ultimate Center of all reality and we in general remain ignorant of this truth.

For most of us Christians, the reality of the indwelling Trinity within us and permeating all of creation as the reason why all creatures live and move and have their being (Ac 17:28) is superficially dismissed as a mystery. We feel a supernatural mystery is something beyond our knowledge and understanding; therefore, it can have no "practical" impact on our daily lives. It simply is a mystery!

Levels of Religious Experience

Even when Christians give verbal acknowledgment to the truth of the Trinity, as Karl Rahner says, the majority of Christians remain "monotheists," that is, they pray to a God who is one and "outside" or "up there."

> . . . despite their orthodox confession of the Trinity, Christians are, in their practical life, almost mere "monotheists." We must be willing to admit that, should the doctrine of the Trinity have to be dropped as false, the major part of religious literature could well remain virtually unchanged . . . Nowadays when we speak of God's incarnation, the theological and religious emphasis lies only on the fact that "God" became man, that "one" of the divine persons (of the Trinity) took on the flesh, and not on the fact that this person is precisely the person of the Logos.

As long as human beings practiced any form of religion or relationships in faith with a Supreme Being, there have been three predominant types. The lowest level we could call *iconolatry*. We build for ourselves an *icon*, a mental image, an idol of God that we adore within our minds as though God is as our projections from within present Him to be. Such a God is easily handled by us through our prayers, rituals and concepts about a fearsome God who somehow or other can be placated in His petty angers by our sacrifices.

14

The second type of religiosity deals with God as a person, or, as in Christianity, three persons in one God. This is a higher level of human consciousness in which God takes on a personality. He loves, judges, pardons, punishes and rewards. He does everything we as persons do, without, however, our human imperfections. There is devotion and loving obedience to God through a person-to-person dialogue. But in the very communication between God and ourselves, is there not also a danger that we project our desires into the person of God so that we end up creating Him according to our own image or at least according to our own needs?

The third level of spirituality has such an exalted idea of God that any idea of Him must be transcended. Dialogue between persons, God and ourselves, yields to *mystery*. In an *apophatic* experience God and we are experienced in an immanent union of two in one where duality yields to subject-subject, one and one make one.

In such a level of Christian spirituality the *oneness* of God and His *threeness* are experienced, not through objective concepts but through the mystery of faith, hope, and love. In God's continuous process of communicating Himself to us unto intimate union, we are to open ourselves to His self-communication as absolute truth and as absolute love within the context of our personal history.

A Revealed Mystery

The mystery of the Trinity has been revealed to us in Holy Scripture. Revelation is a communication, a manifestation of truths by God who makes them known to us. God positively intervenes to disclose to human beings truths by means of signs. And so we can know much about God through His revelation in His created, material world. He reveals more of Himself as a living Person to His chosen people through the Law and the Prophets.

But it is when His Word becomes incarnate that God most fully reveals Himself, no longer in words and signs, but in the one Word and Sacrament, Jesus Christ. We have no way of receiving God's love for us except through receiving the personalized love of Jesus Christ. "As the Father loves me, so I love you" (Jn 15:9).

If God is love by essence, then He is always seeking by His nature to share His being by means of communicating His presence to us. In the Christian religion God becomes a God-toward-others by communicating Himself through His Word in His Spirit of love. God creates the whole world as good, as a sign of His burning desire to give Himself in faithful communication through His Word. The world at its interior is filled with the self-communicating Trinity. God is filling the universe with His loving Self. His uncreated energies swirl through and fill all creatures with His loving, creative presence (Ps 33:4-9). God delights to give Himself through His Word to His creatures.

> . . . I was by his side, a master craftsman,
> delighting him day after day,
> ever at play in his presence,
> at play everywhere in his world,
> delighting to be with the sons of men (Pr 8:29-31).

To The Father Through The Son

God's fullest revelation is made in His Incarnate Word, Jesus Christ, for in Him we have not only words, but we have the one Word that is the perfect copy of God's nature. In Him we can come, not only to know God's very nature, but we can be brought into a loving communion with God's very being through the Risen Lord's Spirit. We can become truly participators of God's very own nature (2 P 1:4). The author of the Letter to the Hebrews describes this revelation in God's Incarnate Word:

> At various times in the past and in various different ways, God spoke to our ancestors through the

prophets; but in our own time, the last days, he has spoken to us through his Son, the Son that he has appointed to inherit everything and through whom he made everything there is. He is the radiant light of God's glory and the perfect copy of his nature, sustaining the universe by his powerful command; and now that he has destroyed the defilement of sin, he has gone to take his place in heaven at the right hand of divine majesty. (Heb 1:1-3)

Knowing the Word Incarnate, we can now know the Father and His Spirit in whom the Word makes known to us the Father (Rm 8:15; Ga 4:6). We, by listening to the Word enfleshed for love of us, can know what the inner life of the Trinity is like. It is through the Word made flesh that we can learn of the communitarian sharing within the Trinity. The Trinity is the model of the same trinitarian energies of love that are shared with us human beings, outside of that essential life of the triune God, that no human being could ever see and live (Ex 33:21; Jn 1:18). We can be caught up into the absolute reality that is at the heart of all other reality, that which is the beginning and the end of all being.

Within The Trinitarian Family

God the Father, the "unoriginated Source of being," in absolute silence, in a communication of love impossible for human beings to understand, speaks His one eternal Word through His Spirit of Love. In that one Word, the Father is perfectly present, totally self-giving to His Son. "In him lives the fullness of divinity" (Col 2:9).

In His Spirit, the Father also hears His Word come back to Him in a perfect, eternal "yes" of total surrendering Love that is again the Holy Spirit. The Trinity is a reciprocal community of a movement of the Spirit of Love between Father and Son. Our weak minds cannot fathom the peace and joy, the ardent excitement and exuberant self-surrender that flow in a reposeful motion between Father and Son through the Holy Spirit. God becomes real only because He can communicate in Love with His Word. His Word gives Him His identity as Father. But that means eternal self-giving to the Other, His Word in Love.

In the very significant words of the French philosopher, Gabriel Marcel, "The *I* is the child of the *We*." We experience our uniqueness only when someone in passover, self-giving love births us into our true being. This is so because we share in God's very own nature. Within the Trinity the *I* of the Father is "birthed" into uniqueness as Father only through the Son and the Spirit. The Son's *I-ness* comes to be only through the gift of the Father in the Spirit of self-emptying love toward the Son. The Father and the Son become unique persons only in being "toward each other" through the kenotic, or self-emptying, love of the Holy Spirit.

Jesus Christ The Revealer

Jesus Christ bridges the abyss of our inability ever to come to know and experience God as He is in truth and love, as He exists, one nature in three distinct persons. There can be no true knowledge of God except through Jesus Christ. "Everything has been entrusted to me by my Father; and no one knows the Father except the Son and these to whom the Son chooses to reveal him" (Mt 11:27).

Jesus speaks the words of God (Jn 4:34). He speaks what the Father has taught Him (Jn 8:28). His words are "spirit and life" (Jn 6:63). Jesus in His humanity is life because He lives by the living Father (Jn 6:57). He is also light and we are light in Him (Ep 5:8) because He comes from the light that is the Father. "Light from Light, true God from true God," as the Nicene-Constantinople Creed expresses it.

What is interior to Christ leads us into the interior of God Himself. He and only He could have become incarnate since He by His nature is the Word of God. He proceeds eternally from the Father in the likeness of nature. The Son has everything He possesses from the Father. He is the expressed image of the Father and so He can bring perfectly to us that likeness of the Father. He is the Word that issues forth from the Mind of God. Hence only the Word is most suited within the Trinity to become the expressed self-realization and image of self-emptying Love of the Trinity.

God's Explosive Love Beyond The Trinity

We can, therefore, see that the ineffable mystery of the Trinity, that escapes our own human comprehension, can, however, be known and experienced in and through Jesus Christ and the Holy Spirit. God not only deemed to reveal the truth of this mystery to us, but in that revelation through the Holy Spirit God has made the mystery of the Trinity available to us through daily experience in each moment of our living situation.

This is what Jesus describes as eternal life. "And eternal life is this: to know you, the only true God, and Jesus Christ whom you have sent" (Jn 17:3). But such knowledge is not merely to be an intellectual assent given to this truth revealed by Jesus Christ through His teaching Church. Such knowledge, in the Jewish sense of the Hebrew word, *yada*, means knowledge of the "heart." It is given to the clean of heart who are promised by Christ to see God, as even indwelling them as in His mansion. This is not knowledge by our own knowing, a knowledge in the darkness of our intellectual powers, but a true experiential knowledge given in light of faith, hope and love, gifts of the Holy Spirit.

This is the "good news" brought to us by Jesus and made possible through the release of His Holy Spirit. We can not only know but also experience the triune God within what Rahner calls the biblical data about the "economic" Trinity. "Economia" (*oikonomia* in Greek) etymologically refers to the well-running of a household. In theology it usually refers to any divine activity of the Trinity in relationship to God's creatures.

Among the Greek Fathers, *theology* properly so-called concerns itself with teaching about the Holy Trinity. The exterior manifestations of God, the Holy Trinity, known in its relation to all created beings, belong to the realm of *economy*. It is such a meaning, namely, the relationships of the Trinity toward the created world, especially toward us human beings, that Karl Rahner states very emphatically in his principle: "The 'economic Trinity' is the 'immanent Trinity' and the 'immanent Trinity' is the 'economic' Trinity."

What does this say to us in our spiritual quest for greater oneness with God and neighbor? This is essentially the Good News preached by Jesus. Love seeks to explode outside, to beget new life in order that the implosive love of the *I-Thou* in a *We* community can be shared and othered in new beings. This is the only Christian explanation of why God has created you and me and has given us the entire created world.

God truly cares for you and me. He not only gives us choice gifts, but He seeks out of His own inner, trinitarian life to gift us with the personalized love of each of the three divine persons in the oneness of their mutually shared divine nature.

Divinization

The divine energies of the Trinity, the personalized love of the Father, Son and Holy Spirit, always surrounding us, lovingly call us to respond to God's Word living within us and within the context of our existential life. We reach our highest development in the continued cooperation (*synergy*) with God's energetic, self-emptying, loving presence.

When we continuously cooperate with God's grace, His divine, uncreated energies manifested to us in the context of our daily lives, we enter into the process of *theosis* or divinization which is the total integration of the body-soul-spirit relationships of man with God. This is the end or goal of God's explosive love in self-giving to us human beings, His masterpiece. We are endowed with an orientation to grow daily into the image and likeness of God that is Jesus Christ.

Intimacy With The Trinity

The unbelievable good news is that the Trinity pursues each of us as the most Tremendous Lover, as the passionate Bridegroom seeks to be one with His Bride. We can truly come to know through the Spirit's faith, hope and love God as personalized Father, Son and Holy Spirit, dwelling intimately within each of us.

Through the Spirit that searches down into the depths of all things, "even the depths of God" (1 Co 2:10), we can experience God as Trinity, giving themselves to us in the deepest and most tender inter-personal relationships. And this is the same Father, loving us as He loves His only begotten Son, His Word, from all eternity within the very Trinity. This is the same divine Word, the Son of God, but also that same Word made flesh and now glorified and risen by the Father. He loves us as He loves the Father from all eternity and as He loved us on the cross. This is the very same Holy Spirit, hidden within the enfolding arms of the Father and Son within the Trinity, loving us with that same bonding love that unites us with the Father and Son, even at this moment in our broken time and space, in our earthly exile.

Our Human Dignity

Do you understand the dignity to which you are called? Do you understand how beautiful you really are right now — in spite of your brokenness and self-centeredness — in the Trinity's indwelling love for you? This is our human dignity: to be called children of God and we really are such by the uncreated energies of God as they touch us at each moment and call us into a more intimate divinization as His children (1 Jn 3:1-2).

This is the Good News that the Word made flesh makes possible through His Spirit who reveals to us in each moment that the full Trinity dwells within us!

21

Chapter Three:

MODERN TYPES OF PRAYER

Many Christians have reached an impasse in their prayer life. There are many reasons for this crisis in prayer. Negatively, activism seems to increase by the day among us Westerners who live mainly in an *animus* culture that measures success by "doing." Such doing activism has for a long time dominated the spiritual life of most Christians. Materialism, that is at the root of the Western way of life, fosters a pragmatism that measures real success by material values and develops a sense of self-sufficiency that contradicts the spirit of the Bible.

Traditional prayer and ritual forms no longer seem adequate to speak to the needs of modern men and women who are in an almost perpetual state of transiency and mobility. The Cartesian dichotomy between mind and matter has all too clearly separated the secular from the sacred, making prayer in the modern marketplace very difficult.

But more positively, such a crisis in prayer has been helped by the growth in personalism within our social order. In a computer society that reduces individuals to statistics and digits, individuals are striving desperately to come forth as persons. There is now a great need for an "I-Thou," person-to-person confrontation not only in one's own personal encounter with the triune God but also in encountering God in the group that assembles for prayer.

Discoveries in the behavioral sciences of psychology, parapsychology and sociology are opening the ordinary lay man and woman to the inner workings of the psyche. Thus, not only are the masses of ordinary people understanding the deeper layers of the inner world that lie hidden and in prayer need to be healed, but they wish to go deeper into their consciousness and unconscious to encounter the indwelling Trinity. Group dynamics and emphasis on building community on the social scenes are providing models for more communal liturgical prayer forms and prayerful living communities in which new formats of prayer are worked out daily.

Expanded Consciousness

Psychologists like Abraham Maslow have coined the word "peak experience" to describe the "ecstasy" or standing outside of our habitual level of consciousness in a new experience. Modern man and woman, as they pray, are seeking new ways of entering into an expansion of their consciousness of identity before their Maker and Lord. Thus what we see today throughout the Western Christian world are many Christians eagerly seeking disciplines and techniques that will allow them admittance into an inner world of contact with the Transcendent or to meet that same hidden God within the group of deeply personalistic, loving persons. Either fed up with the gross materialism of their society or the loss of faith-community in their church affiliation, where they perhaps once had experienced God, they are turning to various forms of Far Eastern meditation, to prayer forms from the Eastern Christian world or merely "Christianizing" forms that come out of the popular quest for positive thinking and expanded consciousness through such movements as bio-energetics, psychosynthesis, Transcendental Meditation, e.s.t., Esalen, Arica, Silva Mind Control and a host of other consciousness-building systems.

Eastern Christianity

Some Western Christians seeking new prayer forms have turned to the Eastern Christian world and found there not only a legitimate Christianity but one that is highly complementary to the heavy Western rationalism both in theology and piety. With enthusiasm such Christians find basically the same doctrines as taught by the Roman Catholic Church and by many traditional Protestant Churches. But what attracts such Western Christians to the Christian East is its rich, mystical traditions. It combines in its prayer forms an admirable synthesis of the prophetic quality found in the Old Testament Judaism with the immediate, immanent experience of the indwelling Trinity that Jesus preached and made available to His followers through the Holy Spirit.

From the desert Fathers of the early centuries of Christianity there came forth an intense form of asceticism and mysticism called *hesychasm*, which means rest or tranquility and can be interpreted in modern language as *integration*. This spirituality aims to bring an individual, through rigorous ascetical practices of fasting, night vigil, psalmody, intense control over one's thoughts and complete openness to reveal all thoughts and inner movements of the "heart" (the deepest consciousness-level, informed by divine grace) to one's spiritual director, to an integration of body, soul and spirit relationships.

The Jesus Prayer

Western Christians can find the practices of prayer and asceticism as taught by this school of hesychasm in the writings of the Fathers of the desert, but especially the writings of the hesychastic Fathers as found in the collection called the *Philokalia*. It is in the *Philokalia* that we find a prayer form called the *Jesus Prayer* that has given much meaning to the prayer life of some modern Christians of the West. In such ancient writings from the Fathers of the desert we discover the prayer as traditionally handed down from their own experience and usage and as they drew it out of what they considered to be the essential message of the New Testament experience of the risen Lord.

At first, the Fathers of the desert repeated it as an oral ejaculation, much like a mantra-chant: "Lord, Jesus Christ, Son of God, have mercy on me, a sinner!" Modern Christians may find that, as they repeat it orally or with the lips, in imitation of the early Christians of the desert, it moves to the mind in silent, intellectual fixation. The highest level of conscious prayer as moving the mind into the "heart," or the deepest conscious awareness of the indwelling presence of Jesus Christ along with the Father and the Holy Spirit, can become also for modern Christians an experience similar to that experienced by the desert ascetics.

Praying the Jesus Prayer

The *Jesus Prayer* can be suited to whatever spiritual development any Christian may find him/herself. It begins with synchronizing one's breathing with the words of the traditional formula, "Lord, Jesus Christ, Son of God, have mercy on me, a sinner," or with some other more simplified "mantra" or fixed word or phrase that will allow the one in prayer to center upon the presence of the Lord Jesus. Some persons use it as a centering technique to enter into prayer, whether it be on a discursive level or on a more advanced, contemplative level of the prayer of the faith. Others will repeat it silently, slowly and with full consciousness of the presence of Jesus during the alloted time of prayer. Others, more advanced, in whom the prayer has become so intertwined with their breathing, will find that the breathing and rhythmically pronouncing of the name of Jesus becomes one with the very heart beat that goes on day and night without any willed effort.

Far Eastern Techniques

Other modern Christians are discovering the healing power of deep, transcendental prayer, found in the prayer disciplines of the Far Eastern religions, such as Hinduism and its various forms of Yoga, Zen Buddhism and the modernized version of Transcendental Meditation (TM) as taught by Maharishi Mahesh Yogi. J.M. Dechanet, OSB Abhishiktananda (Fr. Henry Le Saux, OSB) and Bede Griffiths, OSB are among several Christian leaders who have come from Europe to India and Africa and have tried to create a Christian Yoga by incorporating the traditional *asanas* or postures and breathing techniques as means to free the modern Christian for deeper prayer and lead him/her by disciplined techniques to discover new integration of the broken past experiences into a release of fresh, psychic energy.

Such techniques, they are careful to point out, are not prayer in the Christian sense, but they can be very helpful in preparing us for deeper prayer. The Hatha Yoga postures or asanas, especially the lotus position, can powerfully help a Christian in prayer to withdraw from the disharmonious world of multiplicity in order to "recollect" oneself, to pull oneself to center, and there in humble adoration yield to the Speech of God. Such Yoga offers physiological and psychological aids as preparation for a more contemplative type of listening to God in the tranquility of all one's faculties, as the whole person listens to God in quietness and silence.

One of the important contributions of Eastern Yogic meditation for Western Christians is to offer a corrective against the subject-object separation of the Christian and God. For the Eastern mind contemplating God in the depths of his/her being, the emphasis is on the plenitude of God's fullness and His all-pervading presence. The *Isha Upanishad* proclaims the All-in-Allness of God within the human person so that there remains no place inside the person where God is not: "Plenitude everywhere; Plenitude there, here. From Plenitude comes forth Plenitude and everywhere one with itself there remains Plenitude."

The Hindu *Advaita*, or non-duality, is a theological statement that flows out of an in-depth experience of God as the ocean of being in which the individual floats as a drop. It preserves the mystery that cannot be unravelled through an intellectual process, but which can be approached only in the darkness of paradoxes.

Yogic Concentration

Western Christians are discovering in the meditative disciplines that foster concentration unto "one-pointedness" ways of overcoming the rush of sense bombardment of a noisy, technological world that takes us away from true listening to the indwelling God. Such exercises as suggested by Yoga and Zen Buddhism, as looking intently, for example, upon a flower or a painting until the barriers that separate the subject from the object disappear, can be utilized in Christian prayer. In such exercises a gradual feeling that admits of greater intensity and growth allows the contemplator to transcend the tyranny of one's "conditioned" self and the limitations of place, time and uncontrolled desires.

Through such disciplined concentration the modern Christians can not only begin to perceive the oneness with the world outside but also a slowing down of one's mental activities with an accompanying sense of deep peace and quiet.

Centering Prayer

Carl G. Jung believed that western man and woman would eventually create their own type of Yoga in order to expand their consciousness. He did not see any value in importing the elements from another culture without some adaption to the familiar elements found in Western culture. What has been growing in the use of techniques in modern prayer is the eclectic "borrowing" from a great many sources to develop a Christian type of transcendental meditation, using a Christian mantra drawn from Holy Scripture. This movement does not contradict the interest in the Eastern Christian usage of the *Jesus Prayer*, but it goes somewhat beyond in its openness and readiness to implement elements from any and all non-Christian meditation forms into one which remains quite Christian and centered upon Jesus Christ and the traditional teachings of the Christian Church.

This movement of centering prayer takes on many forms of techniques. The basic belief is a re-capturing of Christian incarnationalism that matter is not evil but can become a meeting place for the divine and the human. The end of such techniques is to become inwardly quieted in order to reach "center" where God and we meet in loving surrender and in total listening.

The Episcopalians, Catholics and Orthodox have always maintained a healthy use of material techniques in their prayer life. Bodily gestures in the Divine Liturgy, the use of bread and wine, oil, holy water, sacraments and sacramentals have always played an important part in mediating God's salvific action.

Catholics have used burning candles, not only to symbolize Christ as the light of the world, but also as a centering technique to move towards the inner center of one's being. They gaze lovingly at the tabernacle, a picture or icon, or a statue, and become centered in the sacred world of God and angels and saints.

Centering prayer is basically, however, a meditation technique that is Christian in its use of a mantra or phrase drawn from Scripture. Fr. Basil Pennington and some of his fellow Cistercian monks of St. Joseph's Abbey in Spencer, MA have developed this Christian centering prayer, using the teaching as found in *The Cloud of Unknowing*. He gives three basic rules to observe in such prayer: 1) at the beginning of the prayer we take a minute or two to quiet down and then move in faith to God dwelling in our depths; and at the end of the prayer we take several minutes to come out, mentally praying the "Our Father"; 2) after resting for a bit in the center in faith-full love, we take up a single, simple word that expresses this response and begin to let it repeat itself within; 3) whenever in the course of the prayer we become aware of anything else, we simply gently return to the prayer word.

Dialogical Meditation

With greater understanding from the field of psychology of the working of the human psyche, Christian meditation has found a new richness through the use of dialogical methods of communing with God. The Bible is filled with stories that show God in dialogue with His people. Individuals in Scripture also are seen as carrying on with God an active "meditation" in dialogical form. When applied to modern Christian meditation the dialogue form of prayer takes one of three expressions: the imaginative, the passive receptive and the quiet, observative dialogue.

In imaginative dialogue the mediator constructs a scene from Holy Scripture by which the participant can vividly place him/herself into the given scene. St. Ignatius of Loyola gives such an imaginative dialogue in his *Spiritual Exercises* for the second and third weeks. Morton Kelsey describes how one can activate the imagination during meditation on Scripture: "In approaching either a parable or an actual event, the secret is to become silent and concentrate on the picture or scene that is presented until it comes to live and begins to move. Then I find that there is a choice. I can stay on the outside and simply observe the action as it unfolds, or I can step onto the stage and become a part of the action. I can even become one of the characters, sometimes sharing in their joy, or often in their agony and pain and then in transformation and victory. It is amazing how the life of Jesus and the parables He told open up to reveal a living, growing meaning with us if we allow imagination to awaken them again and draw us into their reality. They speak at a deeper level than the intellect, touching the total person as intellect seldom can."

Charismatic Prayer Groups

The charismatic movement that developed within the Catholic Church and the other straight-line Protestant Churches out of influences from the Pentecostal, Holiness and Assembly of God Churches in America has given a new group prayer form that most Catholic and Protestant faithful had not known to any marked degree before this movement. Its chief characteristic is exemplified by the charismatic prayer group that meets regularly in order to praise God, receive teachings from Scripture and the doctrines of the Church, and in general to experience the presence of the Holy Spirit as the participants open themselves in genuine sincerity to allow the charisms of that same Spirit to come forth in order to build the Body of Christ.

It is typified by a great deal of freedom in spontaneous praying, sometimes praying in tongues, with free expression given by the participants to personal witnesses of the experiencing of the working of God in their lives in order to praise God in His wonders. Often the gifts of prophecy, healing, discernment of spirits, speaking in tongues with interpretations and the teaching gifts of wisdom, a word of knowledge and understanding may also come forth during the prayer session. Simple group singing interspersing shared prayer will usually reflect some biblical theme that supports the movement of prayer in the group.

Liturgical Prayer Forms

The growth in personalism has seen a movement to develop more communal prayer forms that recognize the individuals in their participation as important elements bringing their contribution to liturgical worship. One modern prayer form that is new for our times but a restoration of a more ancient custom in the Christian Chruches is the restoration of the parish Divine Office where priest and laity come together daily in the morning for morning prayer as preparation for the Divine Liturgy and again in the evening for evening prayer.

With greater emphasis since Vatican II on the solemn proclamation of the Word in the Divine Liturgy, more meditation in silence is being practiced in many parish celebrations after the readings and after the reception of the Holy Eucharist. Attempts to offer forms of greater participation in the Divine Liturgy by the participants in the pews have developed the kiss of peace as a gesture of oneness, more singing of plain and folk music at Masses and the active participation by the laity in reading and leading the congregation in the petitions of the faithful.

Conclusion

We have seen a great richness of modern forms of prayer now being used by Christians as they strive to meet God and each other in deeper consciousness of their unique personhood and that of God and neighbor. Techniques have been restored from the Christian past and new ones have been introduced into modern Christian prayer through contact with the Eastern Christian spirituality and the Far Eastern religions. Psychology and parapsychology have also provided information about the workings of the deeper levels of the psyche in prayer and have prepared the way for new techniques for praying more deeply and less intellectually. The stress on intimacy and community sharing has also brought into the field of Christian prayer new ways of expressing the oneness attained by many in communal prayer.

A final word needs to be said about the use of techniques. A method is good if it works, if it produces the end for which it is used, namely, if it brings us into an adoring union with God. We must keep in mind that what makes any technique or method used in prayer to be truly Christian prayer is that the supernatural grace from God permeates all of our efforts so that our efforts are moving always under the power of the Holy Spirit who infuses into those who seek the virtues of faith, hope and love. Finally we must see that any psychosomatic techniques used must conform to the whole plan of salvation as revealed by the Gospel and Christian teaching through the Church. By their fruits shall you know them to be helpful methods leading us into deeper prayer, greater love of God and others.

Chapter Four:

DISCERNMENT OF RELIGIOUS EXPERIENCES

God has created us to experience His super-abundant, self-emptying love for each of us as revealed in the death-resurrection of His Son. Jesus is manifested to us in the gifts of the Holy Spirit of faith, hope and love as truly being God made man. He lives within us in order to set us free from our excessive attachment to our false ego by living always centered upon the indwelling Holy Trinity. What a struggle it is all our life-time to accept God's invitation to become loving and free and no longer to live in the darkness of self-centeredness!

Feodor Dostoevsky, in his powerful novel, *The Brothers Karamazov*, describes this human struggle to resist Jesus' invitation to be set free by His love. In his legend of the Grand Inquisitor, Dostoevsky describes fictionally how Jesus returns to earth and appears in Seville, Spain in the 16th century. The Grand Inquisitor tells Jesus that He first came on earth to set human beings free, but most of them wanted to live in slavery:

Instead of taking possession of men's freedom, Thou didst increase it, and burdened the spiritual mankind with its sufferings forever. Thou didst desire man's free love, that he should follow Thee freely, enticed and taken captive by Thee. In place of the rigid ancient law, man must hereafter with free heart decide for himself what is good and what is evil, having only Thy image before him as his guide. But didst Thou not know that he would at last reject even Thy image and Thy truth, if he is weighed down with the fearful burden of free choice?

Ignorance and The Will To Power

We modern Christians can struggle for our human dignity and freedom from "foreign," outside oppressors in the arena of politics and economics. Yet in our humble pursuit of greater union with God and neighbor, we can, through lack of solid, spiritual teaching and guidance and a lack of inner discipline and self-control over our own basic inclinations toward sense pleasures and power to control any given situation, become slaves to interior forces.

Christians can stop any well-intended desire for greater progress in the spiritual life by an over-riding attachment to false religious experience. Thus we are in great need of discernment of what experiences in prayer come from God's Spirit and which are from "false spirits."

What Is A Religious Experience?

As you move into a greater freedom to let go under the power of the Holy Spirit, there is the possibility that you can begin to experience physico-psychic phenomena, happenings in the various sense and psychic levels of your consciousness and unconscious. Such psychic and physical experiences can be the seeing of visions and hallucinations, the hearing of voices, the smelling of sweet odors, the feeling of touches from seemingly outside agents, the sensation of enduring, pleasant tastes, paroxysms and physical, violent convulsions, preaching and writing in an "automatic," impulsive manner, levitations or catatonic fixity, swooning or a falling phenomenon and many other related experiences.

The Catholic Church has been very cautious throughout its long history in dealing with both authentic mysticism and "enthusiasm," an exaggerated emotionalism. It knows the power of hysteria and of self-induced physico-psychic phenomena, once the conscious control has yielded to an opening of one's unconscious through mental illness or prolonged introspection as a part of the pursuit of holiness. It also knows the power of demonic forces to communicate and even gain contol over certain physical and psychic areas of a human being's life.

As in all such phenomena that involve a delicate interaction of body-soul-spirit, one can hardly attribute such an individual experience totally to God's Holy Spirit without due discernment, nor attribute it totally to one's own psychic powers, nor totally to demonic control. Discernment is always needed, based on correct teaching. The more a physico-psychic phenomenon has dramatic repercussions upon one's body or physical senses, all the greater care must be taken.

Part of our discernment process is to be sure you know what a religious experience is. Rev. Charles Meyer in his book, *The Touch of God*, approaches the subject of religious experience through what he describes as "human peak experience." "By peak experience we would mean that which is particularly striking and significant . . . and which brings about notable changes in behavior. . . . From a peak experience a person might well develop a whole new outlook on life, a different or more meaningful philosophy" (p. 63).

All of us have experienced such deep experiences, even those in which we did not necessarily feel they linked us up directly with God. To experience God (religiously) is, therefore, one type of peak experience. The "peak experience" has these qualities. It incorporates within itself in some way a union of opposites. It is of lasting character. It contains some element of ambiguity or mystery. It is accompanied by either a heightened or a dulled activity of the senses. It is alogical, namely, it defies a logical explanation while it leads to a new and better integrated view of life. It is more a passive than an active experience. And it is open to a number of different interpretations and evaluations (passim; pp. 64-84).

To the normal peak experience, the specific "religious" experience adds these qualities. It is *numinous* or other-worldly. It is nebulous and may seem obscure or unclear. It is mystical and appeals to the unexplored element of the psyche. It is symbolic, that is, it relates the perceiver through a sign to a deeper reality than the sign itself describes. It is ecstatic or rapturous and, therefore, beyond the world of physical senses. It is liminal, or, in other words, it lies on the border between the world of dreams and the space-time world. And it is "ineffable" and, therefore, cannot be described adequately in any words (p. 95).

Criteria of A Religious Experience of God

With the above as general background, let us put together some criteria to determine whether a "peak" experience is also a religious experience of God.
1. Does the experience integrate itself with sound Christian doctrine?
2. Can the receiver of such an experience better live the Gospel because of this experience?
3. Does the experience give the receiver new purposes or objectives in his/her life?
4. The faith of the subject must be deepened through the experience if it is to be considered authentic. If the experience produces an obsession with itself, it is a negative sign of not being from God's Spirit.

5. Genuine experience of God also promotes a greater child-confidence in God, as well as self-respect and self-confidence. The individual will show greater courage and will not easily be shaken by criticism or rejection.

6. The receiver will experience an increase of love of God which will result in more prayer and in more love for people which will result in a deeper respect for self and all others.

7. Humility is an important sign of authentic religious experience. It is the ability to see oneself more objectively. The receiver will also receive a lasting, deep joy and contentment, a relief from doubts and anxiety.

8. Flexibility and resilience of personality will be another result in one who has an authentic experience of God. An authentic religious experience will release a genuine spontaneity in the personality of the subject. There will be the ability to more fully express one's inner feelings. Thus one will be less inhibited, less self-centered and more inwardly oriented.

9. There will be a decidedly strong movement toward creative work and a strong desire to carry through with such willpower to actuate these desires. Thus the experience will bring pleasure and peace and joy on all levels of one's being.

   Meyer summarizes an authentic religious experience: "Genuine religious peak experience gives a person an opportunity for transcendence while at the same time rooting [that person] more fully both in [self] and God" (p. 99).

10. One important criterion for judging the authenticity of a religious experience is to see whether the fruits of the Spirit, given us by St. Paul in his Letter to the Galatians, are present (Gal 5:22).

11. Another helpful test one can employ is to test the given experience with a past experience that the subject was sure to have been an authentic encounter with God. This would lead to another test: does the subject have a developed sense of God as Someone who is beyond the

subject's control? This test would show itself in prayer as the person yields more globally to the directing force of God over his/her own control during the prayer-encounter with God.

12. A rule of thumb easily applied is to ask, "Is this experience the way God would habitually act, as seen in Scripture and in one's own past authentic dealings with God? Is it similar to what Jesus would do?"

13. A most important negative criterion that would give us a proper conduct toward the religious experience is given to us by St. John of the Cross. Are you separating the physico-psychic aspects of the experience from the spiritual area of deepening faith, hope and love and clinging inordinately to the sense-gratifying aspects? This is all the more common when one experiences powerful "overflow" into our physical and psychic levels which tend to make us want more of such "things" for the gratification to our senses and thrust toward power.

St. John of the Cross gives us this most important guideline in regard to such physico-psychic phenomena:

> And it must be known that although all these things may happen to the bodily senses in the way of God, we must never rely upon them or accept them, but we must fly from them, without trying to ascertain whether they be good or evil, for the more completely exterior and corporeal they are, the less certainly they are of God . . . So he that esteems such things errs greatly and exposes himself to great peril of being deceived; in any case he will have within himself a complete impediment to the attainment of spirituality. (*Ascent of Mt. Carmel;* Bk. II; xi)

St. John goes on to show us that if there is a question of an authentic experience of God, it will produce its effect upon one's spirit at the very moment as it appears or is felt. As God gives these happenings to us gratuitously on His part without any effort on our part, God, therefore, produces in us the effect that He desires by means of such an experience. "It is as if fire were applied to a person's naked body; it would matter little whether or not he wished to be burned; the fire would of necessity accomplish its work" (ibid.).

Fruits Produced In Greater Piety

Because the ultimate criterion, the one Jesus used in the Gospel, of testing any experience by the fruit produced, is so important, I would like to quote at length the important advice of the great 14th-century English mystic, Walter Hilton:

> Beware in that time or soon after and wisely consider the stirrings of your heart drawn from minding and beholding of Jesus and from spiritual exercises and thinking of yourself and your defects or the inward desire of virtues and so, knowing and feeling of God, to set the sight of your heart, affection, delight and rest principally on the said feelings or visions, then this feeling is suspicious and likely to come from the enemy . . . therefore, be it ever so liking and wonderful, refuse it and assent not thereto, for this is a sleight of the enemy . . . But if it so be that manner of feeling makes you more devout, more fervent in prayer and though it be so that it astonish you in the beginning, yet afterwards it turns and quickens your heart to more desire of virtues, increases your love to God and neighbor, makes you more humble in your own eyes, by these tokens you may know it is of God, wrought by the presence and working of a good angel. (*Scale of Perfection*; Bk. 1; pt. 1, Ch. XI)

In testing the fruit of any religious experience to discern what is really of God according to the above mentioned criteria, we must keep in mind that the fruit we are to look for is not necessarily that which can be immediately seen. The ordinary fruit produced from such authentic religious experiences is that which can be tested by time, commitment and perseverance.

Thus spiritual discernment is necessary in such spiritual experiences to see, as we have already said, whether they really are helping to lead us to greater union with God through faith, hope and love, or whether they are obstacles to that union. Psychologists are also interested, where spiritual direction is concerned, not only with what has been experienced in prayer, but above all the manner in which the individual receives the experience and responds to it.

Religion and the Psyche

Karl Rahner has complained of the dichotomy which Western theology and Western Christianity, both Catholic and Protestant, have introduced in viewing God's activities with us. *Nature* is used to refer to what comes solely from human efforts. *Supernature* describes God's special intervention that gives to us a gratuitous power that we in no way possess "naturally." Eastern Christianity, rooted more in the Semitic biblical view of grace, sees God's "uncreated energies" always at work in us and the whole of creation. We are always being gifted by God's presence and His loving energies. These are the Triune Persons in self-giving through divine actions towards creation.

We can speak of God acting in an extraordinary, hence supernatural way, but that might some day be discovered to be according also to God's ordinary ways. Perhaps our lack of understanding of God's immense love and omnipresence in all things causes us to resort to the term *supernatural* to describe God as sole cause.

It is un-Christian to attribute psychic phenomena solely either to a "supernatural" intervention on God's part or a demonic influence on the devil's part. Our Christian theologians, who believe in the Incarnation and the belief that God works in an evolutive manner from matter to spirit, should not be alarmed to think that God meets us, not merely in a direct, spirit-to-Spirit encounter, but also in and through our bodies and our psyches. Our sacramental practices prove that God works on all levels of matter and spirit. It is true that it is ultimately faith that brings us into contact with God. Still God's presence can be felt with powerful effects in the body and the soul.

Psychic Phenomena

Some Christians, especially fundamentalists, have an intrinsic fear of anything that suggests the inner world of psychic phenomena, even though many of them accept and encourage speaking in tongues, prophesy, healing and many other psychic manifestations. Parapsychology has become a legitimate branch of psychology. Its scope is to investigate, with scientific methods, psychic phenomena. "Psi" is a general name for all such phenomena. Some of these would be considered "precognition," a knowledge of a future event before it ever takes place. "Clairvoyance" is extrasensory awareness of external objects or events. "Mental telepathy" allows us to have an awareness of another's mental activities even in distance. "Psychokinesis" is the ability to have direct influence exerted by one's mind upon physical objects without the use of any instruments or physical energy.

Tied to increasing one's psychic powers is the ability to move from a lower level of consciousness into the unconscious to release psychic energies, especially under the influence of a loving openness toward others outside. Can we say God is never working in such phenomena? Can we dismiss any technique that can help us develop such psychic powers as being somehow or other tied to "magic"?

Therefore, we must ask ourselves what is the difference between using such meditational techniques as the Jesus

Prayer, TM, Silva Mind Control, even hypnosis, and true prayer. If in the Christian sense meditation is a prayerful encounter with Jesus Christ dwelling within us, is this the same as hypnosis? The answer to this question will lead us into a very important rule for discerning the proper use of psychic powers and techniques that will increase the development of such powers.

It has been said that all mental techniques of meditation and concentration such as TM, Silva Mind Control, Hindu Yoga, Zen Buddhism, etc. use some form of hypnosis. It can safely be admitted that all such meditational techniques and hypnosis begin with a similar approach: the need to concentrate. It is the beginning point of pulling ourselves away from dispersion into a still point of focus.

The inner motivation is all-important in directing our consciousness once we have reached a state of concentration. True Christian prayer is far from any form of hypnosis. Christian prayer, using similar techniques as those found in hypnosis, Hindu Yoga, etc., does not come under condemnation as being a part of "occultism." In such prayer, the meditator is continually seeking to push his/her consciousness to new levels of awareness of God as "Other" to the meditator, with the resulting acts of adoration and total surrender out of love received and love given in return.

Today God has revealed much about the workings of the human psyche through the discoveries made in depth psychology and psychotherapy. If we are to attain an integrated personality, to harmonize all the various levels of psychic life within our minds, the upper layers of the psyche must be harmonized with the lower layers. This means that the lower layers must be opened up to the scrutiny of the consciousness. We will always remain crippled and be victims of primordial factors in our lives unless we open up these lower layers. The Christian opens up the dark areas of the unconscious in order that the healing power of God's love, revealed by the Word of God, can filter into that broken, demonic world and bring it into a loving harmony and wholeness.

Two Types of Spiritual Experiences

With the general criteria given above to discern true religious experiences from false and this comparison of the use of psychic techniques with true Christian prayer, we can summarize spiritual experiences by dividing them into two classes. One type is an experience in which the "self-image" is preserved. In this type of religious experience you are a free, positing agent, quite in charge as you experience something happening to you, of which you are fully aware. This type embraces all so-called non-unitive experiences which comprise the majority of spiritual experiences.

This type of active involvement on the part of the subject embraces sensory experiences from activating one's imagination. Intellectual insights as an inner "vision" and extrasensory experiences as out-of-the-body experiences and "psi" phenomena would be included in this type.

The second type would embrace spiritual experiences of union. In such experiences all activities, such as thinking, imagining, emoting, become suspended, yet awareness remains open, clear and vibrant. Your "self" seems to disappear. This is habitually present in infused contemplation. But in all experiences, the fruit produced of greater love and adoration of God and greater loving service to others must be the index of such spiritual experiences' authenticity.

Chapter Five:

CONTEMPLATION AS LOVING ATTENTIVENESS

Wherever I go to lecture on prayer or to preach retreats, I meet serious Christians whom God evidently is leading beautifully into the beginning stages of a new manner of prayer that St. John of the Cross simply calls "contemplation." Yet such persons, due to a lack of capable spiritual directors or adequate teaching on the beginning steps into contemplative prayer, tend to become anxious and confused about their level of prayer.

Most of these well-intentioned persons, who already have spent some years in disciplined time of meditative prayer, continually ask common questions that show how perplexed they are and how eagerly they seek solid guidance. One common question asked is: "But am I really praying? I no longer seem to be *doing* anything. Nothing seems to be happening. And, besides, I have much aridity. There are lots of distractions and I feel as though I am wasting my time. Should I not go back to my usual type of meditation on Scriptures?"

Perhaps no Christian master of prayer wrote so thoroughly and so prudently out of his motive to help beginners in contemplation as did St. John of the Cross. In three of his major writings: *Ascent of Mount Carmel; Dark Night of the Soul;* and *Living Flame of Love,* he examines the characteristics of entering into the early stages of contemplative prayer and gives solid teaching to such beginners in a new "knowledge of love," as John defines contemplation.

Meditation

If beginners of contemplation are entering into a new manner of praying, we must see clearly from where they are coming. Meditation in the normal meaning among Catholic teachers on prayer refers to the manner of discursively praying out teachings from Scripture or from the teachings of the Church or the lives of Saints.

Most Christians begin to know God by means of a disciplined form of discursive prayer. This usually consists in taking a page from Scripture, a scene from the Old or New Testament. We go through it, reading it slowly, pondering its meaning. With our imagination, memory, understanding and will, we arrive at some affective presence to God. Our faith, trust and love grow slowly over months and years of such meditation.

As the Holy Spirit infuses these gifts into our hearts, we are able to move from the given text to the presence of God and His divine action. The things, especially, that Jesus said and did, as recorded in the New Testament, become experienced in these prayerful periods. The *where* or the *when* are no longer very important as we enter into the process of letting go of our own control of this historical moment to encounter the saving Lord who transcends the limitations of all time and place.

As your act of faith brings you progressively more and more deeply into the presence of Jesus Christ, His resurrectional presence begins to work upon you. You meet the only

Christ alive today in the event of His person living within you.

A Yielding Presence

As you move into this simple presence of Jesus Christ, a great peace and quietude covers you. Often intense affections surge up with ardent longings to be more intimately united with Him and the Heavenly Father. The consolations in this period of your prayer life can be strong and attractive. God seems to be everywhere, even outside of your period of concentrated prayer alone with God. A global presence of Jesus Christ surrounds you as you begin to find Him in the world around you, in places and persons where you had never "seen" Him before.

You begin to yield with greater susceptibility to His loving presence. Your aggressive activity both in prayer and in your daily actions takes on a gentleness and docility to the indwelling presence of God, both within yourself and within all of creation around you. There is a "letting go" of your power and a new sensitivity, a new listening to God's presence and loving activity around you. You seem to be living on a new plateau of awareness of God's presence. Whether there is ardent consolation or just dryness, there seems to be a deep peace and joy that events, which formerly were disturbing, now do not seem to destroy.

Through the years of meditating on the prophetic words in Scripture, you now have a facility of listening to the existential Word, Jesus Christ, God's Speech, talking to you in the storm that bursts upon you, in the suffering old man before your eyes, the laughing child in play, the traumatic earthquake destroying hundreds and thousands of human lives among your fellow brothers and sisters in a foreign land. You now find that it is God's activity that you are able to perceive and always in the light of a deepening faith that you are loved greatly by Jesus Christ and His Father in their Spirit. There is a sense of growing unity with God and with the world. Anxieties of the moment are surrendered in a childlike trust in God's presence in this or that moment.

A Movement Toward Conversion

St. John of the Cross describes how God usually draws a person into contemplative prayer by what he calls "an enkindling with longings of love." He writes:

> The love of one's Spouse is not the only requisite for conquering the strength of the sensitive appetites; an enkindling with longings of love is also necessary. For the sensory appetites are moved and attracted toward sensory objects with such cravings that if the spiritual part of the soul is not fired with other more urgent longings for spiritual things, the soul will neither be able to overcome the yoke of nature nor enter the night of sense; nor will it have the courage to live in the darkness of all things by denying its appetites for them. (*Ascent*; Bk. I;14,2)

If meditation is the spiritual activity of the beginner, then the "longings of love" represent how the soul is acted upon. The two go together to form a harmonious unity best decribed as sensible spirituality or sensible religious experience. Before conversion the beginner was bound to the world, and his attention, affection, energy and faculties were devoted to wordly things by means of the senses. The beginner does not have faith enough to move away from him/herself to see God as the Source and the Goal of all human strivings.

Conversion brings about new spiritual yearnings. The beginner turns inwardly to find a "new" world. This world always was there but the low level of faith, hope and love did not allow the individual Christian to find God easily in matter. This strong attraction to rest in loving peace and joy in the presence of God brings the first great test for one being called by God to enter into deeper prayer.

This crisis, that all contemplatives must pass through, as St. Paul described it: to put aside the things of a child and to live as an adult, arises simply from this fact. This new attraction that arises in the spiritual part of the person begins to replace the sensible attraction for self-centeredness and soon does replace it completely. The focus of attention, as John describes it, begins to rotate like a compass needle under a greater magnetic force. Attention and energy turn inward, but it is still, however, the energy and natural operation of the faculties that only know how to operate through the physical senses. Therefore, the result is that, in this initial conversion away from worldly objects into a more spiritual world and spiritualized presence of God, the desire for temporal things becomes a sensible appreciation of spiritual matters.

St. John would say that this phase of spirituality with a delightful desiring of sense pleasures in prayer is a necessary stage and serves as "remote" preparation for possible divine union. He writes: "For though the apprehensions of these faculties are not a proximate means toward union for proficients, they are a remote means for beginners. By these sensitive means beginners dispose their spirit and habituate it to spiritual things, and at the same time they void their senses of all other base, temporal, secular, and natural forms and images" (*Ascent*; II; 13,1).

Such sensible delights and fervor become a prime, energizing force of the beginner's prayer life. This explains why at this stage beginners in prayer, despite faults and weaknesses, can devote long hours to prayer and desire greater flight from anything that seemingly takes them from such sweetness.

Purifying Darkness

But such sensible presence of God soon passes. Now a dramatic change happens in the beginner's prayer life. John describes the process whereby God brings the beginner into a self-purification from overeagerness to possess more of spiritual delights. These pleasures are unfortunately filled with much sense experiences reached through faculties that have not yet been purified by deeper faith away from self-absorption.

God leads the person into a purification process that God intends to eradicate from his/her heart the "inordinate" desire for such sensible delights. John writes in *The Dark Night*:

> The reason for this dryness is that God transfers His goods and strength from sense to spirit. Since the sensory part of the soul is incapable of the goods of spirit, it remains deprived, dry, and empty, and thus, while the spirit is tasting, the flesh tastes nothing at all and becomes weak in its work. But the spirit through this nourishment grows stronger and more alert, and becomes more solicitous than before about not failing God. If in the beginning the soul does not experience this spiritual savor and delight, but dryness and distaste, it is because of the novelty involved in this exchange. Since its palate is accustomed to these other sensory tastes, the soul still sets its eyes on them. And since, also, its spiritual palate is neither purged nor accommodated for so subtle a taste, it is unable to experience the spiritual savor and good until gradually prepared by means of this dark and obscure night; the soul rather experiences dryness and distaste because of a lack of the gratification it formerly enjoyed so readily. (*The Dark Night*; I; 9,4)

If you have begun to take the first steps into contemplative prayer, you surely will have experienced how the sensible presence of God passes, being replaced by aridity. As you continue walking along the deeper paths of prayer, eager for greater union with God, you find no longer that sweet presence of God. It is as if you lost Him. The *Song of Songs* best describes your experience in prayer:

On my bed, at night, I sought him
whom my heart loves.
I sought but did not find him. . . .
I will seek him whom my heart loves.
. . . . I sought but did not find him.
The watchmen came upon me
on their rounds in the City:
'Have you seen him whom my heart loves?'
(Sg 3:1-3)

A new presence of God indwelling within you shows itself as darkness. The more that you discover God as loving
Father, the farther God seems away. You have a dull sense of
alienation as you seem to enter deeply within yourself. You
see your own abyss of nothingness before the mountain of
God's majesty. There is a feeling of self-dread with a crying
out in urgency for the face of God. Faith is deepening without the props of sensible consolation, images, words. The
more you advance into this darkness, the more names about
God and His attributes have no meaning. Nothing satisfies
you. The very presence of God that had flooded you both in
deep affective prayer and in contact with the world now
seems utterly absent.

God creates this necessary pruning, this dying of the
seed in order that greater union with Him be possible. You
enter into a necessary dying to your self-reliance and a deepening of faith that only come when you are in this darkness,
standing before a wall that is impermeable to your own intellectual powers.

The Power of Faith

Your prayer now becomes a crying out for God to show
Himself in the night of the desert, where you understand
your own absolute nothingness before God. There is a silencing of your own powers like the silence of steel in the
black night. Only a person who has experienced this trial can

understand because God has been all to this person. And now you have to dig roots and cry out in deep, dark, stark faith for the mercy of God, "Lord, Jesus Christ, have mercy on me!"

Faith for John is seen as a supernatural way of knowing, a gift of God's Spirit. It is a knowing quite different in object and inner dynamism from all natural knowing. No knowledge coming to man through his senses or rational faculties can bring him in contact with God in order that he can know Him as He is. Only faith is the way. God's gift of faith, along with hope and love, transforms us and elevates our natural powers. We must cling to this faith even though this seems to go against our past experiences of knowing through sense perceptions.

Faith and divine union are the two key ideas that allow us to understand what John means by contemplation. In the *Ascent* he uses the image of a pane of glass in the rays of the sun. The more the glass is purified the more it is transformed by the sunlight. It retains its own nature but becomes the sun by participation (2 Pet. 1:4).

Moving Into Contemplation

How can you discern whether God has called you to contemplative prayer? John of the Cross gives us three signs when we are being called to give up discursive meditation and enter into the "loving attentiveness" which he calls contemplation. The first sign is that you cannot meditate with ease as you did before. You no longer experience any sweetness and presence of God as you did in more affective prayer where you were the "doer."

The second sign is that faith has developed to such an extent that you no longer have any desire to fix your attention and thoughts on perceptual knowledge. You easily go toward "center" and find rest there, even without any "sense" feelings and mental concentration.

But it is in the third sign that you are to discover the key of beginning contemplative prayer. The first sign could be the result of lukewarmness, lack of discipline and even sinful attachments. The second sign along with the first might arise through some sickness or general fatigue of mind or body. This is why the third sign is the key indication since it describes the contemplative process itself, so radically different from praying solely with our "minds."

Let me quote in full John's description of this third and "surest" sign:

> The third and surest sign is that a person likes to remain alone in loving awareness of God, without particular considerations, in interior peace and quiet and repose, and without the acts and exercises (at least discursive, those in which one progresses from point to point) of the intellect, memory and will; and that he prefers to remain only in the general, loving awareness and knowledge we mentioned, without any particular knowledge or understanding. (*Ascent*; II, 13, 4, 141)

It is here that you will find your greatest struggle to convince yourself that you truly are praying and in a more intimate union with God than in earlier stages of your growth in prayer. The key to discern whether you have uprooted yourself through God's purifying *night of sense* from being the center of attention and whether now God is your center of "loving attentiveness" lies precisely in this new knowledge or attentiveness to God in "amorous repose." John helps us to discern this new knowledge by another criterion other than our self-centeredness and sense perception of God's presence. "But the more habituated he becomes to this calm, the deeper his experience of the general, loving knowledge of God will grow. This knowledge is more enjoyable than all other things, because without the soul's labor it affords peace, rest, savor, and delight."

We must remember that this state is not one of passivity or general "vacuity," in which we are not involved as persons. Your activity consists now in pushing your will to become more united with that of God, even though there may be extreme dryness and even harmless distractions that cannot be avoided. It is to be expected that as you cease to use your discursive powers of intellect, will and imagination, there will be much wandering of these faculties in search of images and ideas upon which to feed.

Negative Purification

Such prayer of deeper faith has a negative element of slowing down the use of these faculties. A definite purgation process takes place. Even though the thought of God does not necessarily bring any consolation, faith is being exercised in a new way, freed from any ideas or words. John describes the most evident purgation that takes place: "Since God puts a soul in this dark night in order to dry up and purge its sensory appetite, He does not allow it to find sweetness or delight in anything."

Positive Aspect

The positive aspect in contemplative faith that must never be separated from love as you move into a deeper union with God in faith and love is an inexplicable sense of the presence of God, even though on the level of discursive powers He seems absent, i.e., not present merely as He seemed to be to you in meditation-prayer. This is the work of faith and love infused into you through the Holy Spirit who gives you a new interior sense of "seeing" God. It is, as Leonard Boase describes this, like a "sixth sense."

It is a new type of knowledge that has not come by your reasoning powers. It has come as a gift and lies always in deeper, personal relationships between you and the indwelling Trinity.

Totally surrendered to God, you live only for Him as each moment brings you an occasion to be a living gift back to God. A new threshold of union with God has been reached that has passed through the sufferings of the night of the senses. God has taken away from you all attachment to sense pleasures by deepening the faith, hope and love in your heart to make Him the center of your consciousness.

Guidelines

There is so much more that could be said on this important topic of the beginning stages of entering into contemplative prayer. Let me call to mind some guiding principles that may be of help to you.

1. Seek to rid yourself of any anxiety in not praying as you used to. Your work now is to be more intersubjectively attentive in order actively to receive God's gifting of Himself to you in your loving surrender.

2. Through examination of your daily living you will be able to check the authenticity of your contemplative prayer by seeing whether any self-centeredness has slipped into your living out your surrendering love to God.

3. At first your loving attention will demand a more conscious and deliberate attentiveness in prayer and during the day. Gradually this will become unreflective and more yielding to God.

4. A good and experienced spiritual director is helpful in these beginning stages of contemplative prayer. You will progressively experience the words of John of the Cross: "How tenderly You swell my heart with love" (*The Living Flame*; Stanza 4).

Chapter Six:

INNER ATTENTION

If you have ever assisted at the celebration of the Byzantine Liturgy you would be struck by the many times during the Liturgy that the priest or deacon shouts out to the members of the congregation, "Wisdom! Be attentive!" It is a call to become bodily and in spirit attentive, for Christ, God's Wisdom, is about to come into this community in a new and dynamic way.

It is this interior activity of one's mind that is all-important in prayer and in the proper use of all creatures to praise and glorify God. All external activity, unless the mind or heart accompanies it and directs it to God's praise, is useless before God. If your heart, the deepest level of consciousness, is fixed in loving adoration and obedience to God, no enemy can touch you. In fact, then the world of temptations becomes the arena where you, in conflict, can be tested and grow into a deeper, purer love for God.

Need For The Discipline Of Inner Attentiveness

Jesus taught us the end of our Christian life. Yahweh had commanded His chosen people in the desert to love Him with their whole hearts and with all their strength (Dt. 6:5). Jesus paraphrased this same command to be the summary of the end of our human life:

> You must love the Lord your God with all your heart, with all your soul, and with all your mind. This is the greatest and the first commandment. The second resembles it: You must love your neighbor as yourself. On these two commandments hang the whole Law, and the Prophets also. (Mt 22:37-40)

The greatest accomplishment or goal in our human existence is to love God perfectly in every thought, word and deed and to love our neighbor as we would love ourselves. But how often we fail to fulfill these two commands, due mainly to our scatteredness of mind, our inattention to God's loving presence and His Word, asking us always to live in love toward others. What difficulties we encounter when we strive to place God as the supreme center of all our inner motivations and values!

As we understand the greatness of God and His absolute beauty and goodness in His infinite love for us, we will begin to understand ourselves on two levels of existence. We will see the areas of darkness that rise up from within the depths of our hearts that take on a force of aggressiveness as an enemy that attacks us from within the very confines of our inner citadel. We will also see our inner dignity to which God calls us and humbly we will stretch out with great desire to put on the mind of Christ.

Jesus taught us the necessity of inner vigilance and attentiveness. "Therefore, you too must stand ready because the Son of Man is coming at an hour you do not expect" (Mt. 24:44). We are to be vigilant like the five wise virgins who were found waiting when the bridegroom came (Mt 25:1-13). We are to purify our hearts from within for it is there that evil comes forth to make us unclean. "But the things that come out of the mouth come from the heart, and it is these that make a man unclean" (Mt 15:18).

He Himself went against His own will to embrace death out of love for the Father's will (Lk 22:42). And He preached the necessity of giving up a lower level of existence in order that new and more enriching life might come forth from death to the former (Mt 10:39; Jn 12:24-25). St. Paul exhorts Christians to bring every thought as prisoner, captured to be brought into obedience to Jesus Christ (2 Co. 10:5-6). And yet how many thoughts within each hour do we think without referring them to the dominion of Christ our Lord? St. Paul understood the principle of his "unspiritual self" that warred against his spiritual self and he found himself so often doing what he knew he should not do (Rm 7:14-25).

Yet St. Paul knew the importance of disciplining his body in order that he might run to win the crown in the race for salvation (1 Co 9:24-27). He strained ahead and never looked back, all in order to do whatever would be necessary to gain the "prize to which God calls us upwards to receive in Christ Jesus" (Ph 3:14). He described the spiritual life in terms of a warfare, a battle engaged against spiritual forces that are seeking his destruction. God will grant us strength but we must resist the cunning of the devil by taking up all God's armor (Ep 6:10-17). And St. Peter strongly insists on the need for discipline against the attacks of the enemy: "Be sober and watch well; the devil, who is your enemy, goes about roaring like a lion, to find his prey, but you, grounded in the faith, must face him boldly" (1 P 5:8-9).

Sober Vigilance

Taking this above text from the first epistle of St. Peter, the early Fathers of the desert built a teaching about what they termed *nepsis*. This word comes from the Greek word, *nepo*, which means to be sober, not inebriated or intoxicated.

61

It refers to a mental sobriety, a mental balance, an internal disposition of attention to the movement of God's Spirit leading us to true discernment of how we should react to any given situation or temptation according to our true dignity as God's loving children. In this state you are not moved impulsively by your own desires or passions, but you hold yourself in abeyance until you know what this or that thought is all about in God's *Logos*. God is the living criterion of your choices as you seek to act always out of love of God and neighbor. Freedom is not primarily having the possibility of choosing good or evil, but ultimately choosing always the good according to God's *Logos*. This is true integration according to the likeness of God, brought about by fidelity to the interior living Word of God within you.

Self-Possession

Lanza del Vasto, one of Gandhi's disciples, explains how important inner attentiveness is if we are to remember God and seek to return His love by giving ourselves as a gift to others. He writes, "Self-possession must precede self-giving, for one cannot give what one does not have" (*Make Straight the Way of the Lord*, p.8). Such self-possession requires great "spiritual effort." It demands that we attend to ourselves and not to be off center.

Thomas Merton writes in a similar vein:

> If I love God with my heart, I have got to have a heart, and I have got to have it in my possession to give. One of the most difficult things in life today is to gain possession of one's heart in order to be able to give it. We don't have a heart to give. We have been deprived of these things and the first step in the spiritual life is to get back what we have to give and to be ourselves . (*Life and Solitude*)

Attend To Yourself

In my novitiate training I was taught a Latin phrase: "*Attende tibi*," which came originally from St. Basil of the 4th century. We novices were told that meant we were to "mind our own business!" We were not to be curious about the affairs of others. Seriously we were to center upon our rapid climb to sanctity. But it really meant in the mind of St. Basil and all other great ascetics of the early Church that each of us had to cultivate a greater capacity on body, soul and spirit levels for inner attention to the given moment and the task at hand. It is a discipline of the human spirit that allows us to draw near to God so that everything we do is done for His love and not out of our own selfishness.

It is the mind and heart, focused upon God and the goal of the human journey, to love God with our whole heart and our neighbor as we love ourselves. Inner attention drives away any mechanical acting out of routine or a learned response. In a word, we move toward greater human personhood, away from Pavlov's dog which salivated whenever it heard the doorbell ring.

Lanza del Vasto gives us some practical aids to help us attain this necessary inner attention. The first exercise is to help us to rid ourselves of scattered consciousness and our inability to focus on a single thing for very long. We tend to be too much in a hurry and to try to do too many things at the same time. His advice is needed by all of us living in our modern times:

> The first exercise we recommend to you, busy friend, you who have so many important things to do and so little time, will not take you an hour, half an hour, or even a quarter of an hour, but three minutes . . . . And perhaps three minutes is still too much, so let us divide them into six: six times a day, three times in the afternoon, be still. Stop!
>
> You are in a hurry? All the more reason for

checking yourself. You have things to do? Stop, otherwise you will make mistakes. You have to look after other people? All the more reason for beginning with yourself, lest you harm those others.

So, unharness. Relax. For half a minute every two hours, stop! Put down what you have in your hand. Hold yourself straight. Breathe deeply. Draw your senses inward. Suspend yourself before the inner dark, the inner void. And even if nothing happens, you will have broken the chain of haste . . . To recollect oneself is to gather up all the shreds of oneself that were dispersed and clinging to things here and there. Answers as Abraham answered God's call: "Present" (adsum!).

The exercise consists, then, in remaining present to oneself and to God for half a minute . . It is unlikely that in so short a time you will plunge deeply into the mystery of self, but it is not impossible with the grace of God. However, even if nothing else happens during the moment of suspension, we shall at least have broken the chain of events that held us prisoner. We shall have broken it in six and taken the first step toward deliverance.

This exercise del Vasto calls "recall," recalling yourself to yourself. For if we become so engrossed in our work, we really do forget ourselves as free agents, capable of freely moving beyond the demands made upon us from outside of us. He gives us his "perpetual exercise" as distinct from his three-minute one as explained above. This exercise demands that you concentrate your attention on yourself while you are acting. He describes this exercise:

Not just paying attention to the object, to the purpose, to your work, but to yourself seeing the object, yourself going toward the goal, yourself at work.

Which amounts to relating everything to the inner center and centering yourself in what you are doing. It is not enough to pay attention to what you are doing. You must pay attention to yourself doing what you are doing . . . It requires no change in one's occupation or manner, but the sense, the density, the value of all one's acts are wholly changed.

God Speaks His Word

Becoming more aware of yourself as a free agent, capable of putting yourself into your work with the maximum of concentration and creativity is not the goal of your Christian life. That goal we have already described as loving God with your whole heart and with all your strength and loving your neighbor as yourself.

Ultimately you should strive for inner attention so that you can do all, think, speak, act, in oneness with God, in the power of God's Spirit of Love. If God's essence is to be love which means always to be acting in love, as Judaeo-Christianity reveals to us, then He is always seeking to share His being by communicating His presence to us, whom He created according to His image and likeness (Gn 1:26) through His Word. God becomes a God-toward-others by communicating Himself in the gifts of creation through His Word and His Spirit of love. The entire world around us is being created in a process of God's sign of His burning desire to give Himself in faithful communication to us through His Word. The world at its interior is filled with the self-communicating Trinity. God is filling the universe with His loving Self. His uncreated energies swirl through and fill all creatures with His loving, creative, presence. ". . . . Yahweh's love fills the earth. By the word of Yahweh the heavens were made, their whole array by the breath of his mouth" (Ps 33:5-6).

Everything flows out of God's exuberant fullness of being and *becomes* a reality in His communicating Word. This self-communicating God speaks to us constantly, if we are only attentive inwardly, through His word spoken in the oceans and mountains, birds and beasts, flowers and all living things that spring into being under His laughing, joyful gaze. Nothing that is can escape His loving touch, His presence as Giver of life.

God's Logos In Man

Of all the millions of creatures made by God, you and I alone remain unfinished and open-ended as human beings. God speaks to us in the "coolness of evening" in the garden. By our possessing an intellect and will, we are able to enter into communication and ultimately communion with God to share His very own happiness and nature as being love. We can posit ourselves as an *I*, dependent on the Absolute *I* of God, or we can refuse to be attentive to His loving presence. We are being summoned by God continually in every moment of our existence, in each event, to receive God's Word actively. We are called to be listeners of God's Word, to understand and to believe in His Word.

We are not propelled into our uniqueness as individuals by a predetermined guidance on God's part. We are obligated to stand inwardly attentive to God's Word inbreaking into our lives, calling us to respond in faith to obey His Word. He invites and calls us to open our hearts to His Word and to accept our becoming existence in His Word by means of a decision to live according to that Word.

Attention As Resting In God's Word

The language of love is silence. If we are to listen to God's Word, we are in need of silencing the noisiness within our hearts and around us in the multiplied world that is oriented in its brokenness toward "sin and death," symbols of self-centeredness and a movement away from God-centeredness. The condition that served as criterion of one's docility in listening to the Word of God was measured by the early Christians who inhabited the deserts in terms of resting in the Lord or quieting all inordinate desires. Teilhard de Chardin calls such a listening state "passionate indifference," whereby we Christians are to surrender ourselves totally to God in dwelling and revealing Himself within the living temple of God that Christians are called to be.

This state of listening is comparable to the seventh day of rest that the Lord took after His labors of creating the world. It is the new day of rest, the day of *kairos* time of salvation in which we human beings opt always to do that which most pleases the heavenly Father according to His Word. This is described in the Letter to the Hebrews:

> . . . the promise of reaching the place of rest he had for them still holds good, and none of you must think that he has come too late for it . . . . There must still be, therefore, a place of rest reserved for God's people, the seventh-day rest, since to reach the place of rest is to rest after your work as God did after His. We must, therefore, do everything we can to reach this place of rest, or some of you might copy this example of disobedience and be lost. (Heb 4:1-11)

Jesus speaks of the necessity of our entering into our "inner closet" when we wish to pray, and there we are to pray in spirit and in truth to the heavenly Father (Mt 6:6). Scripture and the early Christian writers referred to this innermost self as our "heart." It is into our heart, into the deepest reaches of our consciousness, that we enter in order to come face-to-face in silence with God. In utter openness and receptivity we wait without any preconceived ideas of what Jesus, the Word of the Father, will reveal to us from within us and from without, in the world events around us of this new day.

God's Exterior Communication

A general emptying of our own driving, aggressive attacks upon God, others and the world around us and a putting on of a gentle spirit to listen to God as He communicates Himself to us are necessary if we are to be in touch with God as He communicates Himself to us both from outside and from within ourselves. A disciplined inner attention is needed if we are to be ready to hear what God's Word is saying to us.

God reveals Himself through His Word as found in Holy Scripture. This requires a listening on the levels of body, soul and spirit as God's message comes to us as history, an intellectual message to us. Then God's Spirit speaks not only a special healing word of love in the broken time and space in which we listen to this word but He also releases the dynamic power of God that gives faith and hope in God's will to fulfill what His Spirit reveals.

We approach listening to the Word of God in Scripture with humility and gratitude, but, above all, with childlike faith that God's Word made flesh is still with us unto the end of the world in His revealed Word (Mt 28:20). Yet it is always a fresh, new Word being given to us as we listen with complete inner attentiveness and in deep faith, hope and love. Such listening to Scripture is not merely a dry study, an intellectual exercise, but it is a heart-to-heart encounter with Jesus that demands great inner attentiveness.

Such listening means that we also are listening attentively to God in His revelation within the Church in its authority to teach and preach God's Word from Scripture and from the living traditions developed continually as the hierarchical members teach with their special charism the other members of the Church.

68

Attention To God In Other Persons

A special listening with attention to God's Word as an unfolding of God's loving presence is developed as you learn to listen to God in others. Here you can see from your own experience what inner attentiveness and love are required if you are truly to listen to God in the presence of other persons who meet you and communicate themselves to you through their words, actions and their very being. At first, we listen on the bodily level to God's Word speaking to us through others. We seek to praise God in the positive qualities found in them. We can observe negative qualities also in others, but we seek to move from the bodily level into a faith, hope and love vision that will allow us to pierce beyond the evident negative side of the person to see deeper the Word of God and to listen to what message of beauty and love the Word is speaking from within that person.

The greater our awareness of the indwelling presence of God in the deepest center of our being, the greater we will become conscious of this same divine, loving presence surrounding and penetrating all other things. Gone are the anxious, aggressive moods to dominate each situation to satisfy our physical and psychic needs. A new global sense of God's presence is discovered in each human encounter as we push aside the veils of the externals to enter into the inner, loving presence of God. As we become freed from our false *ego*, the screaming lies and suspicious doubts about our own identity and that of others, we can remain humble and loving, gently looking into the eyes of each person encountered to see there the face of God, shining through as Love in the unique gift of the other person.

Attentive Prayer

God does meet us and communicates Himself to us more directly in our own personal prayer. The more attentive we can bring ourselves to His activities in self-communication unto communion, the more "real" He becomes to us. We cannot love and surrender to Someone who is not real to our consciousness. It is distractions that take us away from intense intimacy with God.

Distractions are anything on a body, soul or spirit level, that enter into our communication and communion with God. Voluntarily or involuntarily willed by you, they can prevent you from being attentive in faith, hope and love to God. Distractions tend to dissipate your attention away from God and, therefore, defeat the prime purpose of prayer: to lift your mind and heart up to God in loving surrender and adoration.

Most of your distractions in prayer will be involuntary. Especially, as you move away from discursive prayer and do not employ your intellect, imagination and memory as much in your contemplative resting in God's loving presence, distractions will come as a plague. When such seemingly carry you away from the focus of God, gently but firmly move back into the faith orbit by centering upon God's presence and what you are about in your prayer.

Only by returning to inner attention in prayer and in all you do for love of God can you fulfill St. Paul's exhortation: "Be happy at all times; pray constantly; and for all things give thanks to God, because this is what God expects you to do in Christ Jesus" (1 Th 5:16-18). Thus your will always becomes one with God's will. This is to obtain the goal of your life: to love God with inner attention and in complete surrendering love.

Chapter Seven:

DISCERNING GRATITUDE BY COMMITMENT

Have you ever noticed how great a part of your life is spent in giving thanks to those who have given gifts to you? Our lives would not be fully human without persons showing us their love and commitment in the gifts they give us. And how very spontaneous it is for us to be moved with gratitude when friends shower us with gifts!

Thanksgiving is an essential part, therefore, of our human love-relationships and also basic in our prayer-relationships to God. The reason why one who receives favors from others offers thanks is that a relationship of love and a sense of belonging are established whenever there is a giver, giving a gift to a receiver.

The psychology of gratitude and commitment to God and friend is clearly expressed when a young man gives to his fiancee a costly diamond ring. The man acts out in symbol his desire to give his whole life in a committed union to that woman by his gift of the ring. The fiancee accepts the gift with great joy and gratitude and gives her "yes" in a returned commitment.

This is why our prayer-life is so full of praise, gratitude and commitment to God. We reflect on God's outpoured love through the unending number of gifts He gives us at all times. Behind the symbol of each gift God wishes to give Himself to us in a committed covenant of faithful love.

True Gratitude to God

In true gratitude to God we wish to return thanks, not only by expressing in words our gratitude, but also by our inner disposition of our heart (the scriptural term that represents the human person of emotions, intellect and will, permeated by God's grace of faith, hope and love). St. Thomas Aquinas shows that gratitude is measured by the disposition of our heart. "Sincere kindness depends on the heart rather than on the deed, so, too, gratitude depends chiefly on the heart." (*Summa Theologiae* 106; 3; ad 5).

Thanks given in the Bible is primarily a response to freely offered gifts of God to His human children. We are exhorted over and over in the psalms to give thanks to God for all His gifts to us. "Let these thank Yahweh for his love, for his marvels on behalf of men. Let them offer thanksgiving sacrifices and proclaim with shouts of joy what he has done" (Ps 107: 21-22).

In the Old Testament, there is no single Hebrew word to correspond to our word *thanks*. To show gratitude to God for His many gifts the people of God joyfully *praise*, *bless* and *glorify* God. Joyful praise to God is an essential part of expressing our gratitude to God for His many gifts.

Praise God

The very last Psalm 150 summarizes an essential element of thankful prayer to consist of a cosmic hymn of praise:

Praise God in his Temple on earth,
Praise him in his temple in heaven,
Praise him for his mighty achievements,
Praise him for his transcendent greatness!
Praise him with blasts of the trumpet,
Praise him with lyre and harp,
Praise him with drums and dancing,
Praise him with strings and reeds,
Praise him with clashing cymbals,
Praise him with clanging cymbals!
Let everything that breathes praise Yahweh!

Other examples of prayer of praise are found in Pss. 19; 46; 93; 96; 100; 103; 135; 145; 148. St. Francis of Assisi continues this gratitude as praise to God in his famous *Canticle of the Sun:*

O most high, almighty, good Lord God, to Thee belong praise, glory, honor, and all blessings!

Praised be my Lord God with all His creatures; and especially our brother the sun, who brings us the day, and who brings us the light. . .

Praised be my Lord for our sister the moon, and for the stars, which He has set clear and loving in heaven

Praised be my Lord for our brother the wind, and for air and cloud, calm and all weather, by which Thou upholdest in life all creatures.

Praised be my Lord for our sister water, who is very serviceable unto us, and humble, and precious, and clean.

Praised be my Lord for our brother fire, through whom Thou givest us light in the darkness. . .

Praised be my Lord for our mother the earth, which doth sustain us and keep us, and bringeth forth diverse fruits, and flowers of many colors, and grass.

Praised be my Lord for all those who pardon one
another for His love's sake and who endure weakness and tribulation. . .
Praised be my Lord for our sister, the death of the
body. . .
Praise ye, and bless ye the Lord, and give thanks
unto Him, and serve Him with great humility.

Prayer of Thanksgiving

Psalm 138 is a model of so many other psalms, canticles
and recorded prayers of thanksgiving in the Old Testament.

I thank you, Yahweh, with all my heart,
because you have heard what I said.
In the presence of the angels I play for you,
and bow down toward your holy Temple.
I give thanks to your name for your love and faith-
fulness; your promise is even greater than your
fame.
The day I called for help, you heard me
and you increased my strength.
Yahweh, all kings on earth give thanks to you,
for they have heard your promises;
they celebrate Yahweh's actions.
"Great is the glory of Yahweh!"
From far above, Yahweh sees the humble
from far away he marks down the arrogant. . .
(Other psalms of thanks are Pss. 33; 40; 65; 66; 166;
136).

Gratitude in the New Testament

In the New Testament, we often meet Jesus expressing
thanks to His Father by praising Him (Mt. 11:25; Lk 10:21).

In His last supper discourse He turns lovingly toward the Heavenly Father to glorify and praise Him for what the Father has done and will be about to do in His life (Jn 11:41; 17:1-f).

Jesus expected thanks to be returned by the ten lepers whom He healed (Lk 17:18). But He was disappointed when nine of them did not return gratitude to Him. Acknowledgement, praise and thanksgiving to God for benefits received is a most basic element of all Christian religious acts and is at the heart of true prayer and worship.

St. Luke (Lk 6:35) replaces the phrase, "the just and the unjust" of Mt. 5:45 with the phrase, "the ungrateful and the selfish." Some of the Pharisees and the Scribes gave exterior thanks to God (Lk 18:11), but they were not made righteous by their prayers of thanksgiving since their hearts were focused through pride upon themselves and not humbly upon God, the Giver of all good gifts (Ja 1:17).

Thus we can violate gratitude by defect when we fail to return thanks to God for His abundant gifts. We can also offend against gratitude if we were to thank God as though He helped us in our pride and selfishness to perpetrate any form of evil out of selfishness and pride. The Pharisees and Scribes offended against gratitude by not giving also themselves as a gift in love to others as a result of God's gifts given to them.

Pauline Thanksgiving

St. Paul gives us in his writings a theology of thanksgiving. How often he exhorts the early Christians to return thanks to God for His fidelity in committing Himself to serve them through His gifts. "Be happy at all times; pray constantly; and for all things give thanks to God, because this is what God expects you to do in Christ Jesus" (1 Thes 5:18). Again St. Paul pours out praise, blessing and thanks to God for the inestimable gift of the Christian calling:

> Blessed be God the Father of our Lord Jesus Christ, who has blessed us with all the spiritual blessings of heaven in Christ.
>
> Before the world was made, he chose us, chose us in Christ, to be holy and spotless, and to live through love in his presence, determining that we should become his adopted sons through Jesus Christ for his own kind purposes, to make us praise the glory of his grace, his free gift to us in the beloved. . .
>
> (Eph 1:3-6)

Nearly always in his letters St. Paul inserts an expression of thanksgiving to God after the initial greeting, e.g. "First I thank my God through Jesus Christ for all of you and for the way in which your faith is spoken of all over the world. . ." (Rm 1:8-ff). Constantly he writes genuine and spontaneous prayers of thanksgiving. He insists that giving thanks to God is a duty for Christians that is accompanied by rejoicing as God's gifts are recalled to mind (1 Thes 5:18).

Paul exhorts Christians to express thanks in action. This action is best performed in communal worship (1 Co 14:6-ff). Christians are not only to offer thanks to God for the favors they themselves have received from God, but also to offer thanks and petitions for all human persons (1 Tm 2:1).

Christians, for St. Paul, are to be "givers of thanks" (Col 3:17). We are to abound in thanksgiving (Col 2:7) because of the superabundant graces we have received from God (2 Co 9:14). But with thanksgiving there must be also joy (Col 1:12).

The Sacrifice of the Mass

The best prayer of thanksgiving we can offer is to praise God in the sacrifice of the Mass. The word, *Eucharist*, in Greek means "the giving of thanks." In the fourth eucharistic prayer of the Roman Mass, immediately after the consecration, the priest and people pray for the Church: "By Your

Holy Spirit, gather all who share this one bread and one cup into the one body of Christ, a living sacrifice of praise."

The third eucharistic prayer begins with these words: "Father, You are holy indeed, and all creation rightly gives You praise." An essential part of each Mass relates somehow in the various prayers to the ancient Christian hymn, "Glory to God in the highest. . . we praise You for Your glory." Even as we now praise and thank God for His infinite glory and goodness to us, so we look forward to Heaven to continue this praise for all eternity. In the fourth eucharistic prayer we pray: "We shall sing Your glory with every creature through Christ our Lord, through whom You give us everything that is good."

Thus praise and thanksgiving necessarily go together and are never separable. In the Mass we are privileged to receive from the heavenly Father through His Spirit of love His only begotten Son as God's perfect Gift to us. But we are also privileged to return to God our perfect gift of Christ, our Brother, along with our individual and ecclesial gift inserted into the Body of Christ, our Head. The arrangement of the Mass expresses the fact not only of an exchange of gifts between God and ourselves in Christ, but also the commitment unto self-sacrifice that is the essential part of the Mass. God in the Mass gives to us His Word, the scriptural teaching. We give to God our offering of thanksgiving and praise in and with Christ. God gives to us the eucharistic Christ as the sacrifice poured out on the cross of Calvary and as the sacrament of love given for the life of the world in the Communion between the Trinity and ourselves.

We give ourselves as a thinking gift when we go forth from the eucharistic oneness with the Trinity to be eucharist to others in loving service. Here we see how thanksgiving to God for His greatest Gift of Jesus calls us to respond to be not only a gift of thanksgiving to God but also a committed child of God, one with Christ in His Spirit, to seek always to obey the Heavenly Father's will.

And we know that God's constant will is that we love one another as Jesus loved us. This we are able to do now only if we allow Jesus in the Eucharist to transform us into a loving oneness in His Spirit. Through His Spirit we are enabled to go forth in committed love and service to others in the world around us.

Living in the Heart of Christ

As Christians who have understood through the Spirit of love the infinite love of Jesus for us, we will strive to live more and more consciously in that union with Christ effected in the Eucharist. Jesus is to become a "Living Bread," a guiding force directing us from within. "Think of the love that the Father has lavished on us. . ." (1 Jn 3:1). If Jesus, the Lover of mankind, the *Philanthropos*, so full of love for you, truly abides within you, becomes your praise, glory and blessing toward the Father, how can you fail not to be praise, glory and blessing toward others? Eucharist or thanksgiving is never completed unless there is also committed response in loving service toward God's other children.

No matter how difficult it may be to be committed to lovingly serve those around you, you now have the constant source of true gratitude and commitment living within you. He gives you courage to become one with Him in all that you do and think and say. You can accomplish infinitely more than what you could ever do alone ". . .for cut off from me you can do nothing" (Jn 15:5). Peace and joy of the Spirit of Jesus govern all your thoughts, words and deeds because you have experienced in the Eucharist the infinite love of God.

This love is not very far away, but abides within your very *heart*, your deepest consciousness, through the gifts of the Spirit of faith, hope and love. No force outside or even within from your unconscious can harm you ". . .because you are from God and you have in you one who is greater than anyone in this world" (1 Jn 4:4).

In spite of your weaknesses and the darkness and sin in your "members" (Rm 7:23), your Lord and Master dwells within you. "Make your home in me, as I make mine in you. As a branch cannot bear fruit all by itself, but must remain part of the vine, neither can you unless you remain in me. . . Whoever remains in me, with me in him, bears fruit in plenty; for cut off from me you can do nothing" (Jn 15:4-5).

A Living Worship Unto God

We have seen how praise and thanksgiving to God arise as a spontaneous movement of prayer toward God, the Giver of all good gifts. Praise comes easily to your lips as you touch the myriads of creature-gifts bestowed upon you by a loving Father of us all. You find yourself praising God for the beautiful gifts of nature, food, drink, clothing, health, friends. You find yourself also praising Him even in times of trials and sufferings for the same Spirit convinces you that all things work unto good for those who love the Lord (Rm 8:28).

But you and I know how easily verbal praise comes to our lips. It isn't everyone who says, "Lord, Lord!" who will enter into the kingdom of God! It is those who keep the Lord's commandments who really become a praise and expressed gratitude to God.

Ultimately all prayer—petition, propitiation, thanksgiving— leads to adoration and worship. This flows out of a sense of wonder, awe and mystery as we stand before God in our inner poverty of spirit, overwhelmed by the grandeur and power, but also the tender intimacy of God toward us in His loving service. Worship is an act whereby you relate yourself to ultimate meaning found in complete surrender to the sovereignty of God.

Worship, as thanksgiving, never ends after the last word of praise dies on our lips. Worship, thanksgiving and commitment only begin as the love of God impels us outwardly toward our neighbor in loving service. True gratitude and adoration for God will engender the strongest love for others. There is only one source of true love, divine or human, and that is found ultimately in the Trinity. To be a Christian who prays is to be a person of continued *eucharistia*, of thanksgiving to God, proved by one's commitment to Him to obey His commands of complete loving service to God and to neighbor. What else is there to committed love?

Chapter Eight:

SPIRITUAL DIRECTION THROUGH A SPIRIT GUIDE

Have you asked yourself recently, "Is it necessary for me to have a 'spiritual director'? What would such a guide do for my spiritual life? And just where would I find such an 'extinct species' of the human race?"

Since its beginning, Christianity has always lived with the hope of being one, loving community in Christ; one family—the family of God. We all share this longing and are aware that we really belong to such a community, the Church, the Body of Christ. It is only within the Church that new life can begin to grow and take on the form of the fullness of Christ and the transformation of this world into a loving family of human persons in Christ. It is within the Church that the Holy Trinity manifests itself. By participation in the very trinitarian life in Christ and through His Holy Spirit, we human beings can realize our full potential of being made participators of God's very own nature (2 P 1:4).

The place of the spiritual director or spiritual direction as an art must be above all anchored squarely within the Church. This has always been understood within the Catholic Church. It is so basic to Christian spiritual direction that

81

the tendency to speak of spiritual direction, guidance by the Holy Spirit through the "conduits" of other human persons, outside of the Church and God's historical revelations of truth, would be absurd.

The fundamental truth is implied as expressed by the Russian theologian, A. Khomiakov. He writes: "We know that when any of us falls he falls alone, but no one is saved alone. He is saved in the Church, as a member of it and in union with all its other members." St. Dorotheos of Gaza of the 7th century clarifies this principle: "We need assistance, we need guidance in addition to God's grace. No one is more wretched, no one is more easily caught unawares, than a man who has no one to guide him along the road to God. It says, 'Those who have no guidance fall like leaves.' Leaves are always green in the beginning. They grow vigorously and are pleasing to look at. Then after a short time they dry up and fall off, and in the end they are blown about by the wind and trodden under foot. So is the man who is not guided by someone."

Spiritual direction and the Church are complementary since their aim runs along many parallel lines. Both draw unto themselves from common sources of revelation through Scripture and tradition the great truths that make up Christianity. Both find in the sacraments the living encounter with the risen Lord and Savior. Both need the discernment of spirits as guided by the teaching authority in the Church.

What is Spiritual Direction?

A generally accepted definition of spiritual direction could be expressed as such: Spiritual direction is the art of leading individual Christians to their proper perfection according to their personal vocation and their place in the Church. It is a form of pastoral care practiced by Jesus and His New Testament followers in a "pre-conscious" way. It evolved and flourished in the early centuries when infant Baptism was the norm and the rite of Christian initiation of adults was in decline and the sacrament of reconciliation was received only for the gravest of sins. Lay confession of sins was always practised and various rites, such as the Eucharist itself, had always been the sources of God's forgiveness. Yet people have always felt a need for guidance in their spiritual development. They discovered among the laity and the clerical or religious groups certain men and women who had a charism of discernment of spirits and could lead them into greater freedom to become uniquely their true selves and to be capable of discerning the workings of the Holy Spirit in their own lives.

Pope Leo XIII, in his encyclical, *Testem Benevolentiae* (1899), condemned the view that the guidance directly of the Holy Spirit was sufficient for a perfect Christian life. He insisted that the exterior teaching authority of the Church and the sanctifying action of her ministers is necessary to complete the interior action of the Holy Spirit.

Pope Pius XII, in his encyclical, *Menti Nostrae* (1950), stated that without spiritual direction from a "prudent guide" it is often very difficult to be duly responsive to the impulses of the Holy Spirit and the grace of God.

Traditional Model

Basically we have seen within the Catholic Church two models of spiritual direction. The first is the model prevalent until Vatican II and can be characterized by the following description. The director is usually a priest or someone with a special office in the Church, e.g., a novice mistress or master of novices. Such a director has been given this position in an official or quasi-official capacity and has received some special technical preparation for this office.

His/her function is not only to guide souls and resolve certain important questions, e.g., in the choice of a vocation, but especially to form in the guided ones some special, appropriate way of spirituality which is assumed to be willed for them by God. Such "formation" is carried on according to a preconceived system. Individual differences are to some extent to be respected but it is the system and the form according to the "spirituality of the institute" that receives major emphasis. This is seen in most third orders of laypersons formed by a priest of a given religious order. Often such direction is given through the sacrament of reconciliation or "the manifestation of conscience." The director is seen as one who has all the answers. The "subject," like a child, obeys the director without much personal dialogue.

Soul-Friend Model

To speak today of a spiritual director or a spiritual "father" suggests to most of us moderns a paternalism and impersonalism that all too often reduces the directee to an "infant," docile and obedient, even to the whims of the director. With growth in personalism and a grounding more solidly in Scripture, we find a more preferred model for relationships between the director and directee. This is much more ancient than the traditional model described above. It has its roots in the Christian East. Such early spiritual directors were called "pneumatophors" or "Spirit-bearers" since they strove to be led as perfectly as possible, not by their own discursive powers, but by the immediate illumination of the Holy Spirit. They sought to become purified instruments so that the Spirit of the risen Jesus could unveil the plan of God for the individual seeking direction.

They sought to become purified instruments so that the Spirit of the risen Jesus could unveil the plan of God for that individual. They were humble servants, filled with love of God and neighbor, who sought to aid others in becoming the individuals, the true selves, that God wished them to be. Listening to the Spirit operate gently in the lives of those who came for spiritual direction was all important and not their own answers to questions posed by the pupils. The first principle, therefore, in this model and in all true spiritual leadership must be that the spiritual guide be deeply grounded in God in order that the Holy Spirit could effectively speak through him/her.

Thus spiritual direction no longer is conceived of as the special province of a priest or religious by virtue of an "office" bestowed upon him/her or by virtue of having studied theology. We can see that this is a broader view of spiritual direction and can apply to the role of a good, loving parent as well as a trusted and experienced friend who in intimate conversations or by letters makes valued suggestions, giving encouragement and inspiration which aid one in spiritual progress.

The relations of the one directed and the director are informal, perhaps even in some sense casual. Yet it is clear that one is receiving guidance and help from the other. There is a distinct relationship of "spiritual filiation" in a broad sense. There is no question of the one having formal authority over the other. The director according to this model discreetly and informally conveys to the directee the knowledge of a certain spiritual "way" but not necessarily in a logical, systematic manner of teaching. What is important is the uniqueness of the directee and discernment as to what the Spirit is doing to guide him/her in the most "appropriate" manner for that person's growth in human freedon.

The director is conceived as exercising a divine and spiritual action in the life of the one directed. Listening with the heart to the directee's description of how the Spirit has been guiding in that person's life is all important.

Modern Psychotherapy and Counseling

To determine more specifically the unique role of Christian spiritual direction we need to distinguish it clearly from modern psychotherapy and counseling. Many times all three may be undergone by an individual and in all three one can discover the loving operation of the Holy Spirit to bring that person to a richer life in the Trinity. Yet each discipline has its own specific goals.

In *psychotherapy* the process originates in some painful experience, of a mental or emotional illness. The role model is medical with the psychotherapist functioning as a doctor or healer. The relationships operative are those of a healer and a patient. The dynamics of the relationship deal with restoration of health, mental attitudes and emotional behavior. The process is terminated when there is achieved freedom in emotional balance and mental health allows the patient to make normal contact with the here and now.

Counseling focuses upon a problem experience of ignorance or confusion. The role model is pedagogic, that of a teacher who clarifies and imparts knowledge. Hence the operative relationship is that of a teacher toward a pupil or learner. The goal of the process centers around the solution of the problem with ignorance being dispelled or confusion dissipated. An example would be marriage counseling or career counseling. The process is terminated with the resolution of the problem and the discovery of skills, e.g., to find direction to follow a satisfying career.

Christian *spiritual direction* employs a process built around a promise experience. Through revelation God has revealed His promise by words spoken and lives witnessed. The role model is that of an already initiate, a holy person, who has already lived or discovered how to live out in daily *praxis* what right teaching revealed by God has manifested. Therefore, the relationships operative are those of a holy person and a disciple as well as God in relationship to the disciple. The process is one of awakening another to new awareness and a sense of direction is discovered. The process never in this life reaches a termination but the given relationship may be terminated for various reasons of a pragmatic nature.

Broader Forms of Direction

Within the last ten to twenty years many Catholics have moved away from the general form of spiritual direction in the sacrament of reconciliation as the exclusive "place" for receiving the guidance of the Holy Spirit through a "teacher-director" and even beyond the formal one-to-one of the traditional concept of spiritual direction to discover spiritual direction in new and more personal ways.

Marriage Encounter taught millions of Christians how married couples could dialogue with each other and discover the Holy Spirit directing both of them to greater, loving union between themselves and as a unity with God.

The Cursillo Movement brought an individual in an "intensive" weekend experience to a new and personalized relationship to Jesus Christ and taught him/her how to share in a small group and with a "co-pilgrim" to examine weekly one's relationships with Christ. The Charismatic Renewal through the weekly prayer group sensitized Christians, "baptized by Jesus in His Spirit" to a new freedom in that Spirit. It opened up Scripture as a "place" to encounter God's spiritual direction, but also to find the direction of the Holy Spirit in a communal charismatic prayer service, focusing chiefly upon praise of God and individual healing of body, soul and spirit relationships.

Various renewal programs in parishes opened up the ordinary Catholic in the pews to the dynamic, Spirit-filled teachings of Vatican II. Thus we view today spiritual direction primarily as the work of the Holy Spirit who labors at all times to set us free from our crippling, sin-laden brokenness in order to be "divinized" into beautiful persons, loving God with our whole heart and our neighbor as we love ourselves.

Three-Fold Relationships

Spiritual direction has as its goal primarily to enable the directee to achieve a deep relationship with or grounding in God, and thus to live a life of total freedom, individuality and deep love. Therefore, while the relationship between the individual directee and God is primary in spiritual direction, there are also two other relationships that help in obtaining the goal of the first. These are the loving-concern for each other between the director and the directee and then the relationship of the director with God. In another teaching we can develop the first and second relationship, namely, God and the directee and the director and the directee. Let us now develop the relationship of the director with God, since it touches radically the other two sets of relationships.

The Relation Between the Director and God

In philosopy there is the saying, "No one can give what he/she does not possess." How very true this is in the case of spiritual direction. The guide must lead the directee in the "ways of God" by prayer, instruction and example. Perhaps one's living example is the most important influence upon a beginner in the spiritual life or upon one who is advancing but needs the example and encouragement of a director who has gone before in his/her personal experiences of the dynamics of growth in the spiritual life.

The first quality sought in a spiritual director is *holiness*. As the directee is still not perfect in all ways of the spiritual life, he or she needs the mediation of a holy person, man or woman, to bring forth new "birthings" in the Holy Spirit. Only one who has already passed through ascetical purification and has arrived at a certain, habitual union with the indwelling Trinity brought about by the Holy Spirit can recognize the workings of the Spirit and properly guide another along the same path.

It is clear that the director must personally and continually be experiencing the dynamics of the spiritual life in order to understand what the directee is undergoing. St. John of the Cross lamented often about directors who lacked personal holiness and experiential knowledge of the spiritual life. He quotes Matt. 15:14 in this regard: "If a blind man leads another blind man, both fall into the pit."

Only an experienced holy person can understand that "pat" answers to fit all cases in the same way will never do in good direction. The director must be so in touch through docility of the Holy Spirit as to what response is to be given in the greatest love toward God and the directee, that he/she allows the Spirit to move freely and use the director as a pure conduit through whom God's graces will pass into the directee.

The holiness of the director through his/her continued union with the indwelling Trinity will bring about a holy model for the directee. Love and peace and joy will radiate from the director and the directee will see a living example of what he/she can become with God's grace and still become God's unique child. Part of being a model to the directee will consist in creating an ambiance for the directee of the Spirit's peace and harmony. This will help the directee to have hope that in his/her confusion, there can be a way out into greater integration and harmony.

Holiness of the director will also show itself outside of the actual periods of direction as the sanctity and love of the director will be a powerful force of intercessory prayer on behalf of the directee who at a distance may be undergoing great trials and temptations. With such prayerful grounding in God as his/her center, the director will not be swayed by the many psychic and spiritual forces that can often be released in such encounters during a direction-session. Directees can often employ subtle ploys and game-playing. Only a humble, holy person can remain a mirror through which the directee can recognize such tactics and deal with them openly.

Learning is an important quality for a good director. Such knowledge should be not only of theology and the right teachings of Christian revelation, but also of the operations of human psychology and the science of the unconscious. St. Teresa of Ávila writes: ". . .but if he [the spiritual director] is not a learned man, this lack of learning will be a hindrance. It will be a great help to consult with learned men. If they are virtuous, even though they may not experience spiritual things, they will benefit me."

Humility is especially necessary for directors since they are to put the directee's interests before their own. A proud director will seek in a strong *animus* nature to subjugate and dominate the directee to do the will of the domineering director.

Together with humility two most important qualities must be sought in a good director: prudence and charity. Holiness and experience are greatly to be desired, but these alone without learning, prudence and humble discretion may be useless, or even lead to great harm.

Seeking a Spiritual Director

Pray to God to lead you to such a good director as we have outlined here. Inquire from spiritually developed persons whether they know of any such director. Seek in him/her a good listener, a contemplative, calm, loving, humble, holy and learned person. Look for one who is moving freely with the Holy Spirit and takes a prophetic stance between God and the world. Arrange a meeting with the person, after you have been open to finding a good director, not exclusively in a priest. A laywoman or layman, single or married, a religious nun or brother may be able to guide you during the present phase of your spiritual journey. The director need not be for the rest of your life!

Remember, true leadership in the spiritual life can only be measured by the spiritual leader's surrender to the complete guidance of the Holy Spirit. It is only in true love that we can experience God as actively loving us and bringing us into a transformation to be love to others.

Chapter Nine:

RELATIONSHIPS BETWEEN DIRECTEE AND GOD AND DIRECTOR

The true director in spiritual direction must always be the Holy Spirit. We must never oppose spiritual to material. Spirit is opposed only to the sinfulness of self-centeredness. This what St. Paul calls in Rm 8:7-17, "the flesh" or *sarx* in Greek.

Let us examine first in this teaching the fundamental relationship of the directee with God, since God is concerned with all levels of our human existence—body, soul and spirit. God is now creating us unto His loving children according to His very own image and likeness (Gn 1:26) that is Jesus Christ.

Directee In Relationship With God

This is the primary relationship and goal of all spiritual direction. The other two relationships, namely, between the directee and the director and the director and God are very important if this most primary relationship is to grow. All activities touching spiritual direction must be subordinated to the individual's free following the Spirit of God. New knowledge is given to you directly by God in your prayer. Healing of hurts and dispelling of darkness from self-centeredness and laziness and fears touch most intimately your living relationships with God, Father, Son and Spirit.

We can see here the fundamental difference between psychotherapy and spiritual direction. In the former the relationship between the therapist and the patient is the focus for healing and growth. In spiritual direction any progress comes from the individual's struggles with God and his/her surrendering to His loving will.

The director must always be secondary as a mid-wife, catalyst and privileged witness to aid in releasing God's life in the directee. God alone is the true spiritual director. The director serves the directee to align him/her in harmony to do God's will in any given situation.

The director is like a sign post, helping the directee to find the shortest and most direct way "home." But it is always the directee who must walk with his or her own two legs in the ways of the Lord. Thomas Merton writes: "Get thee gone, and sit in thy cell, and thy cell shall teach thee all things! . . . . this clearly implies that there is no use in the monk leaving his cell and running about asking advice, if he is not first prepared to face his own solitude in all its naked reality" (*The Spiritual Father in the Desert Tradition*; p. 100).

Desert Purification

No matter how great the depth of the spiritual director, your growth is determined by your willingness to plumb the depths of your own heart and to enter into an aloneness with the Alone, God. It is in the desert of your heart that you will have to strip yourself and come face to face with who you are and who God is in your life.

Kenneth Leech describes this desert, so necessary for one's growth in spiritual perfection:

> The desert—the real desert—bears in its physical reality the signs of isolation not only from people and human life, but from any semblance of man's presence and activity. Being something that man cannot put to use, it likewise bears the sign of aridity and consequently of the subduing of all the senses, including both sight and hearing. It also bears the sign of poverty, of austerity, and of the most extreme simplicity. In short it bears the sign of man's complete helplessness as he can do nothing to subsist alone and by himself in the desert, and he thus discovers his weakness and the necessity of seeking help and strength in God (*Soul Friend*, p. 142).

To the beginner this may appear frightening but for one who burns with the desire to encounter the living God and be transformed into Him, no cost is too great. On the contrary, it is one's willingness to be purified, to lay bare one's hidden wounds that begins the healing process.

If anything is to be gained from spiritual direction, so much will depend on the depth to which the directee is willing to open up his/her heart. This deep hunger and ardent faith seem to be the key in determining the fruitfulness that will come from spiritual direction. Openness and transparency mean much more than just having a facility for expressing one's inner thoughts.

A Unique Relationship With God

You form a unique relationship with God and this must be constantly consulted in spiritual direction. Neither the director nor you as the directee can know the end result of your unique and most personal relationship with God. You, as one who receives spiritual direction from a director, must be asked continually by the director, "What is God calling you to do in this particular circumstance?"

Freedom to be one's true self is one of the main goals of every person's spiritual journey. Therefore, there cannot be imposed upon you, the directee, any timetable for your spiritual growth. At times you may not be ready to move ahead even though the director may think that is the way to go. At times there will appear periods of stagnation and aridity and even a retrogression on your part.

The director may foresee that you are moving toward a "dead end" and would like to save you time. Yet you might need to experiment and even seemingly "fail" in order to come to a better understanding of how God is leading you and of your weakness and strengths.

Developing Discernment

In the beginning stages of your spiritual life, you will need a director to help you discern between the movements of God's Spirit and your own "spirits" which come out of the self-centered levels of your psyche and not out of your true self on the spiritual level of obeying God's Word.

You will develop through the help of your director the ability to interiorize yourself and to learn experientially which voice or "spirit" is operating and on what level of your inner psychic and spiritual life. The main contribution of the director is to help you sensitize your listening and discerning faculties so as to be in "attunement" with God's will.

As you develop the "sixth" sense of knowing how the Spirit operates and what fruits He brings forth as you cooperate with His guidance (Ga 5:22), you will broaden your discovery of spiritual direction in wider ways than chiefly through the agency of a spiritual director.

Often the Spirit speaks through our ordinary circumstances of life. People near you, seemingly dropping a word, a suggestion, recounting an incident, even a dream, can prepare you to hear the Spirit. Here you should test each new message so it does not contradict God's previous ways of working in conformity with Scripture and the teachings of the Church.

Spiritual discernment becomes a constant attitude of openness and sensitive docility to God so that you may at all times walk in freedom of being a child of God and choose to act in all circumstances in ways most pleasing to your Heavenly Father.

Directee And Director

A third and important element in spiritual direction is the close and loving relationship between yourself as directee and your director. This relationship is never to be solely a relationship between a teacher and a disciple. The director can never be only wise and independently detached from any openness to share himself/herself with the directee. The director must be humble and open to receive also from the Holy Spirit through the intimate and loving interaction with the directee.

The real beauty of the spiritual experience lies in the mutual growth in the life of the Spirit that is experienced both by the directee and the director. In such a loving community of mutual openness to the same Spirit operating, both the director and the directee grow, if they seek to be open. In the beginning of the relationship between the directee and the director, the directee usually is on the receiving end. But as the directee matures in the life of Christ and in discernment of spirits, he/she should grow in confidence and a sense of awareness in following the way opened by the Spirit.

A director who is truly sensitive and open will have great reverence and respect for the unique way that the Spirit is leading the directee. A true director never seeks to impose his/her way as the only way, but is filled with a great liberty of Spirit and seeks only true, deep inner peace for the directee. The director always looks for the fruits of the Spirit in the directee which is a sure sign of His presence and the fact that the directee is following the will of God.

Ideally, you and your director should touch the core of the other's being, the place where God unites both of you in the trinitarian love. Ignace Lepp writes of the value of having such a spiritual friend:

> To meet a master who wishes to become our friend is a great opportunity in life. Thanks to him/her we shall be able to actualize our principal powers to the maximum. The man who has confidence in himself, far from refusing to be a disciple, freely chooses the master he/she believes most suited to help him/her become himself/herself. If there is an art of being a master, there is also an art, scarcely less difficult, of being a disciple. The most effective masters generally began by being excellent disciples. Even Christ began by being baptized, and therefore initiated by the Precursor.

Mutual Help To Each Other

This is the understanding of a "soul-friend" as understood in early church spiritual direction. The close relationship between the "elder" and the disciple is grounded upon the deepest movement of the Spirit, binding the two into a loving relationship that goes far beyond any other relationship known in human love, since both persons are striving at every moment to be guided totally by the same Holy Spirit.

The saints were such soul-friends to those who came to them to share the workings of the Spirit in both the director and the directee. Such spiritual guides were utterly uncalculating in their self-giving and caring for those whom they sought to help in the spiritual journey. They show us that spiritual direction involves something more than answers to problems, pious cliches and ready-made remedies that were supposed to fit most human beings without consulting the uniqueness of God's working in one's life.

It must be realized that the directee also can help and comfort the director. The latter can hear the Spirit directing him/her through the uniqueness, enthusiasm, generosity, etc., of the directee. However, the director must never intentionally seek to "use" the directee and thus reverse the roles so that the directee begins more to direct the guide.

This union of love demands the acceptance of the other in all his/her uniqueness, including idiosyncracies and failings. Such love through the Holy Spirit goes beyond any ordinary human inclinations and capacities. It can operate with divine grace where there might be a basic difference in temperament. An unconditional love between the director and directee is a most important element to successful direction. It is in the milieu of such reciprocal loving concern that deep healings and subtle direction by the Spirit occur.

Here are some guidelines for a spiritual director (remember, we are called to help others grow in greater perfection and, therefore, God can use all of us in the role of a director) in relationships to the directee.

Helps And Guidelines

1. If you are the director, keep all relationships between you and the directee always subordinate to your own personal relationship to God.
2. Be always centered upon God and open to the guidance of the Holy Spirit throughout the entire conversation.
3. Keep the tone and your conduct such so that the directee feels free and comfortable with you.
4. Be cautious about any affection shown you. The other's relationship to God is primary. If after some time of getting to know the directee there is evidence on his/her part or both of you or even only from your part that there

is a growing affection and strong attraction for the other, this feeling should be looked at in a prayerful manner and proper precautions taken so as not to impede mutual docility to the Holy Spirit.

5. Be quick to notice the manner in which the directee presents a given problem. Look for signs of consolation and desolation as well as content of the problem.

6. Do not push the directee beyond his/her capacity or level of spiritual progress.

7. Avoid giving your own advice to the directee or telling exactly what he/she must do. Let the directee go to prayer to discern the movement of the Holy Spirit. Your approach or experience of how to "solve" the problem may not be that of the Holy Spirit and, therefore, not good for the directee.

8. Normally speak sparingly and only after mature reflection.

9. Give advice only on the way in which the other can discover God's will and not on what God's will for him/her could possibly be.

10. Seek always to bring the directee into the deepest presence of the Trinity and, therefore, easily to move into prayer.

11. Be attentive to subtle ways that the directee may, either consciously or unconsciously, seek to project upon you a certain unhealthy role that might indicate a harmful transference.

12. Beware of "pontificating" and showing off your knowledge in certain areas that might be side-tracks to the immediate task at hand. Move the conversation always back humbly to the Lord.

13. Do not hesitate to disturb the peace if this is necessary.

14. Like Mary Poppins, do not seek to give excuses for a situation which the directee thinks is wrong. Let him/her remain in darkness until he/she can see the light.

15. All sorts of emotions and feelings will arise during a conversation. Learn to bring them into a prayerful presence to God.

Direction With Discernment

Much more could be written about these three relationships, so central to Christian spiritual direction, namely, the relationship of the individual directee with God; the relationship of the spiritual director with God; and the interrelationship between the spiritual director and the directee. There may be and certainly are many skills and tools which are important for both director and directee to possess in the relationship of direction. Yet behind all of them, and presupposed by the relationship itself, is the ability to prayerfully distinguish between the actions of the good spirit and the evil spirit, and further, to interpret the movements within the person, whether they be from within the person or from outside.

To enter into spiritual direction without this important tool is similar to trail-blazing without a guide or compass. Since each direction-situation is unique, dealing as it does with the individual and his/her life, this discernment must be a living, flexible approach, nothing text-bookish or statically legalistic.

However, strangely enough, there are discernable patterns in the spiritual life, just as in other endeavors, and these patterns when linked to the given case, provide the basis of the discernment of spirits, which we have detailed in a previous teaching. Perhaps the re-occurrence of these patterns is not so unusual after all, if we consider the following.

First, we are creatures with a nature, individually and uniquely forming us into a person so unique that there is no other in all of creation quite like us. Yet we enjoy a common nature with a common end, which is the eternal, exciting, joyous *theosis* that through the Trinity's uncreated energies at work in our lives leads us into a sharing in God's very own divine nature by grace (2 Pe 1:4). Yet there is also opposition from the evil forces at work in the cosmos around us and within us.

Second, these forces of opposition, and "evil" itself, are not creative, but parasitic, imitative in a grotesque mode.

99

Being a perversion of good, rather than anything in and of itself, evil cannot have the infinite multiplicity and endless, delightful originality of God and His goodness. The Cosmic Dance is one of order and invention, pattern and spontaneity. Evil merely mocks and sneers, piping a dull drone of no value. This may help to explain the surprising regularity of the attacks on the spiritual pilgrim.

From regularity, rules may be devised. As we have pointed out in an earlier teaching, St. Ignatius has given us a set of "Rules for the Discernment of Spirits" which, far from being a tedious or pietistic exercise, are vital and surprisingly accurate guides for the director and directee.

Direction With The Christian Community

Lest we might think that spiritual direction unfolds only through two people, the director and directee, with God vitally involved as well, we need to point out in conclusion that all true spiritual direction comes out of the Body of Christ, the Church, and is oriented toward the building up of that Body throughout the world community. Spiritual direction never is solely vertically related directly to God and ends there. The spiritual life of Christians never distinguishes between a personal, private life and one's public involvement. All of our lives unfold and are actualized within a living community of persons. We must always seek to know God's will and what He wishes us to be and do in relationship to our fellow beings.

The true aim of those seeking the will of God in prayer and in spiritual direction is to bring God to the world and the world to God. When we love one another, God's love is being perfected in this world (1 Jn 4:12).

Chapter Ten:

DISCERNING CHRIST'S SECOND COMING

Could you honestly say that, in the wake of so many recent devastating earthquakes, the Middle East wars, the rampant crimes committed everywhere on our streets, the increase of world terrorism, the threat of unemployment facing many workers throughout the world, you haven't wondered at least whether we are nearing the end of our created world?

As a Christian, you have undoubtedly believed for a long time that this earth as we know it will one day reach its end. You have recited the *Creed* that professes faith in the second coming of the Lord Jesus to this earth in glory to judge the living and the dead. But perhaps you have been too practical minded to worry too much about the details. You have too many other problems to solve so why worry about God's problem of ending His creation?

Various Approaches

Yet, as we reach the end of the second millennium of our Christian era, the year 2000 is becoming a focal point for various speculations about the impending future. One group of speculators concerning the future of planet earth is that of

101

the *futurologists*. These are the economists and other scientists who are looking seriously at the resources of our earth in order to foresee the future needs and to plan now for their attainment. Alvin Toffler defines such "futurists" as a "growing school of social critics, scientists, philosophers, planners, and others who concern themselves with the alternatives facing man as the human race collides with an onrushing future" (*The Futurists*, p. 3).

Such futurists see the future as an unfolding of the potential locked within the earth's resources that can be developed to bring forth a richer world if human beings cooperate in a logical manner. The future is seen as a fruition much as an oak tree is the growth from an acorn. The process is a "becoming" of what is already there.

From right wing Christian Evangelicals there comes an evergrowing "new apocalypticism" that differs radically from the futurists. They base their future prediction, not on a becoming, but on a coming, the *coming* imminently of Jesus Christ. They are the promoters of "the boom in doom," as *Newsweek* called this type of stepped-up Christian speculation about the end of the world. Their books abound in book stores with titles such as *The Late Great Planet Earth*; *The Terminal Generation*; *God's Plan for the Future*; *The Vision*; *You Can Know the Future*; and *What on Earth's Going to Happen?*

The most outspoken latter-day prophet of right-wing Christian apocalypticism is Hal Lindsey who pinpoints the end of the world in his book, *The Late Great Planet Earth*, to come imminently "within forty years or so of 1948." The New Apocalypticism derives its knowledge of the terrible destruction of the earth and the signs of the second coming of Jesus Christ, not from the authentic sayings and parables of Jesus Christ, but from an insistence upon a literal fulfillment of the apocalyptic sayings found in the Old and New Testaments.

A Christian Eschatology

And, yet, throughout all of Christianity there has been a happy mingling of the tension between a becoming of the potentialities locked within our earth and a coming of Christ. A true sense of the apocalyptic, the yearning for the fulfillment through the sudden intervention of Jesus Christ to put an end to the sufferings of this world and to bring final judgment to the just as well as the wicked, has always been an essential part of this authentic Christian eschatology (which means the study of the *end times*). The Bible promises a transformed humanity and a cosmos through the cooperation of human beings working under grace with God's imminent and creative presence in all of matter.

The term *apocalyptic* is derived from the Greek word *apokalypsis* (Rv. 1:1) that means an uncovering or a revealing. It refers to that type of literature that bears this name and is mainly concerned with revealing what has been hidden. It can be used in several meanings. Basically it refers to a group of writings with common characteristics mostly developed in the last two centuries BC through the first century AD. Then it can denote ideas and concepts that are found in such apocalyptic writings.

Pure apocalypticism never was a good carrier of the Good News that Jesus came to bring us. Christianity is a Gospel of hope. It preaches the power of the past in which God has repeatedly shown His mercy, especially in His Son, Jesus Christ, who died for all mankind. It proclaims also the importance of the present moment in which to receive the Spirit of the risen Jesus and co-create this present world into a new earth and a new heaven. But it also predicts the coming back to this earth in glory of Christ and a final judgment and restoration of all things in Him to the Father.

The Return Of The Lord

If apocalypticism is a poor vehicle for conveying the basic truths of Christianity, it still has an important element to contribute to the preaching of Christianity. Primitive Christianity eagerly looked forward to the coming of Jesus imminently. In the New Testament we do find apocalyptic language used. However, the writings of the New Testament are not to be considered as a part of the strictly so-called apocalyptic writings mentioned above, based on specific ideas, chiefly on prediction in history of what will infallibly happen when certain signs occur that foretell the second coming back to this earth of the long-awaited Messiah. We can indeed find in the New Testament individual sayings of Jesus and His followers, especially the author of the Book of Revelation and St. Paul. Such apocalyptical language, as found in Mark 13, Matthew 24, Luke 21, 1 Corinthians 15, 2 Thessalonians 2 and Revelation, provides the authors with a language framework of reference that was well known both to Jesus and His followers of the first century. It was not meant to disclose historical, future events about the end of the world so much as to give exhortation and instructions to the readers of such writings as to how to act now in the present moment that would lead the Christians to the final end of the world.

Millenarianism

Millenarianism is the teaching which holds that, before the second coming of Jesus Christ in judgment, He will return to this earth to establish an earthly kingdom that will last literally for 1000 years. The word is derived from the Latin word for 1000, *mille* and *annum*, year. Scripturally it is based on the text of the Book of Revelation 20:1-15 which teaches that Satan will be chained for 1000 years and that the martyrs and those faithful to Jesus will come back and reign with Him on this earth in a messianic kingdom.

Such literal interpretation of the Book of Revelation's text has been held in the early Church by a few church Fathers, but, in general, such a teaching has been condemned as heretical from the time of St. Augustine to the present time.

The Rapture

It is this teaching that is broadcast so constantly on TV fundamentalistic programs, advocating the theory of pre-tribulation "rapture." Based on a faulty interpretation of the Greek word used by St. Paul in 1 Thessalonians 4:16-17, such teaching holds that Jesus will come suddenly and catch His chosen ones up in a rapture, taking them into the sky without a moment's notice. Those who are left will be subjected to great tribulations. Hence the dispensationalists work out a teaching on the rapture taking place before any sufferings can be inflicted upon the true believers of Christ. Therefore, the rapture is "pre-tribulation." The rest of the world will suffer, but not the "chosen ones" whom Christ has selected to be "raptured" out of the sufferings and tribulations inflicted upon mankind.

According to this erroneous interpretation Christ will come in two phases. The "rapture" will precede the coming of Christ with His resurrected ones and all true believers will return with Him. The "rapture" will be the first resurrection of the true believers who will be taken up with Christ into glory for a seven year marriage with the Lamb of God. During these seven years great tribulations will take place on earth. The Antichrist begins his terrifying reign, but eventually the Jews will turn to Jesus and He will come in glory accompanied by His disciples to destroy His enemies in the final battle of Armaggedon.

Such teaching must be rejected in the light of the 2000 years of Christian interpretation and because its teachers fail to do full justice to the entire Old and New Testament revelation. Its naive literal interpretation of selective prophecies and an unenlightened tapestry woven out of texts drawn without any regard for the historical context which exalts an elite group of self-righteous Christians who will not suffer any tribulation while the majority of other human beings will receive the wrath of a vengeful God totally ignores the full messages of God's revealed Word.

A New Earth And A New Heaven

What is the destiny of this world that God, when He created it, as reported in the Book of Genesis, saw that it "was very good" (Gn 1:31)? Scripture guarantees to us that God is involved in a process of evolution, in which He, with the cooperation of us human beings, is engaged in transforming this material creation into "a new heaven and a new earth" (Rv 21:1). God never creates to destroy but only to transform into something that will give Him greater glory as it reflects the unity brought about by His loving activity within matter.

This present earth, that knows so much of disharmony and evil, division and separation, is meant by God's eternal plan to enter into a fulfillment, a recapitulation and reconciliation of all things to His original plan. This is very much the vision of St. Paul in his breathtaking vision of the role of the cosmic Christ recorded in the letter to the Colossians:

> He is the image of the unseen God and the first-born of all creation, for in him were created all things in heaven and on earth; everything visible and everything invisible . . . As he is the beginning, he was first to be born from the dead, so that he should be first in every way; because God wanted all perfection to be found in him and all things to be reconciled through him and for him, everything in heaven and everything on earth, when he made peace by his death on the cross. (Col 1:15-12)

The work of Christ is nothing less than to redeem the entire created order by bringing it together into a unity, into a sharing in His Body, the Church. This is the proper understanding of the Old Testament prophecies that speak of not a literal 1000-year period of harmony before the tribulations and destruction of the universe, but of a final reconciliation of all created things by Christ to the Father. In Is 65:17 and

Rv 21:1 we read about a new heaven and a new earth. St. Paul and the early Fathers understood this as the biblical way of referring to the completion of the entire universe.

A True Christian Understanding

The true Christian vision of the incarnation and resurrection of Jesus believes that by assuming a material body, the Word made flesh inserted Himself into the heart of God's created cosmos. By His death and resurrection, Christ, in His gloriously spiritualized humanity, is now present to the cosmos in a new manner. He is directing the movement along with the cooperation of us human beings in history and the completion of God's creation toward *Omega* when there will be only Christ. He will be everything and He will be in everything (Col 3:11).

In a real sense, the *parousia*, the final appearance in glory of Christ, is already present in our universe. He is not coming as though He has never been here. He is working to transform and bring into completion the entire created world. This world belongs to Christ, not Satan! He is now achieving in process the victory over cosmic evil, a victory that will be full and perfect at the end of time. In those in whom Christ is now living, there flows the same eschatological life He will live in them in the second coming. He is now overcoming the forces of death, sin and disorder by bringing about a gradual transformation in the final *parousia*.

Now, about this last stage, this final transformation. God did not deem it necessary for us to know all the details. Fundamentalists, who appeal to the description of a gigantic cosmic cataclysm, bringing an end to this material world, fail to see the Jewish apocalyptic imagery and the deeper meaning in the passage "The Day of the Lord will come like a thief, and then with a roar the sky will vanish, the elements will catch fire and fall apart, the earth and all that it contains will be burnt up . . . when the sky will dissolve in flames and the elements melt in the heat" (2 P 3:10-13). What will be burnt up will be the sinfulness and disharmony, and righteousness will reign through a transformation of what was imperfect to what will be perfected in Christ Jesus.

If God were to annihilate the present cosmos, Satan would indeed have won a great victory. God never creates to destroy but only to transform into higher forms of unity and uniqueness of each creature taking its place in the total Christ. As citizens of God's kingdom, we cannot write off this present earth as a total loss only to be destroyed nor can we rejoice in its deterioration. This is to deny the incarnation and the fundamental truth that God not only sees matter as good but that He has inserted Himself through Jesus Christ into each atom of creation and is working from within to bring all things into a new creation.

We have a grave responsibility as we live on this earth, not to run away into a far-future, heavenly region and cop out in the meantime from our duty to work with God's plan to co-create this earth into God's Kingdom. With St. Paul we should see Christ as an immanent, indwelling force, actively working, suffering, rejoicing, growing in the cosmos of God's creation. Christ is here and now being formed in His Body.

Building The Body Of Christ

We are members of His Body and each of us has a role to play in the reconciliation of the cosmos to Christ's power and the completion of the potentiality God has locked inside of all creation unto His eternal glory (2 Co 5:17-19). In order to find Christ reconciling His cosmos and to be actually able to cooperate in His cosmic redemption, we must turn within ourselves daily and hear the Spirit of Christ guiding us.

In purity of heart and humility we are to see the uniqueness of ourselves, given talents by God which only we can develop with God's grace to add something unique to the building of Christ's Body. We are in need of a constant "conversion," a turning toward the indwelling Spirit to be guided by the values of Christ.

As we turn within ourselves daily in prayer and purifying reflection that heals us of our selfish love, we find Christ more easily in our material involvements and work. We yield our talents to His direction. We seek to live according to God's inner harmony found in each event. We become His servants as we lovingly work to serve others. It is possible by God's grace after much prayer and purification and loving service toward others to live and move and act out of a conscious love for God in the most profane situations. Without detracting from our full concentration on the given tasks at hand, our work can be the environment, a *divine milieu*, in which we adore and serve God who infinitely loves and serves us in Jesus Christ and His Holy Spirit.

God is asking us not to worry about the "end times" and the details of the second coming of Christ; rather we are to work to build the Body of His Son into its fullness. He is already present and inserted into matter. There can be no greater humanizing force in our lives than to work consciously toward this goal. For we have been created to be according to His image. We are continuously in process, through our daily lives of activities and passivities, joys and sorrows, sin and reconciliation, of being divinized into God's loving children by becoming one in His only begotten Son. As we know ourselves in the Father's eternal love, we become the extension of His Son's Body, to bring others by our love and God's love in us into that Body.

Then God's eternal plan will be completed. God will be found in all things. But in the meantime God challenges us in the commission given to us by His eternal Son, Jesus Christ: "Absolute authority in heaven and on earth has been conferred upon me. Go, therefore, and make all nations your disciples . . . And mark: I am with you at all times as long as the world will last" (Mt 28:18-20).

Right Teaching—Right Living

What does this topic about the "end times" have to do with your personal prayer-life? There is a simple law in the spiritual life that is the key to a right understanding about the end of the world. The early Greek Fathers were unanimous in their realization that *orthodoxy* (*orthodoxia*) or right teaching and *orthopraxis* or right practice go together.

Simply put, Christians must rightly believe in God's revelation about His nature and His relationships to us and His created world, about our human nature and the end or purpose of our creation and that of the entire material world. If in our prayer, we are convinced of God's eternal plan for us and this cosmos of ours, then in our daily living, in every thought, word and deed, such solid God-revealed truths will be our directing force.

We will obey Jesus who still exhorts us as He did while He was on this earth: "But regarding that day or hour no one knows, not even the angels in heaven, nor yet the Son, but only the Father. Look out, be wide awake! You do not know when the moment arrives. It is as when a man goes abroad: on leaving his house he gives his servants their authority, assigning to each his special task, but he directs the doorkeeper, in particular, to keep awake. Remain awake, therefore; for you do not know when the master of the house returns, whether late in the evening or about midnight . . . What I say to you, I mean for all. Remain awake!" (Mk 13:32-37).

Discover answers. . .

. . . in LIVING FLAME PRESS books

Today's Christians have many questions to ask — questions on prayer, spiritual growth, suffering, unity, living as a Christian in today's turbulent society. Living Flame Press offers some answers, bringing you books by such prominent authors as George A. Maloney writing on spirituality, David E. Rosage on prayer and meditation, Robert Lauder on the challenge of Christian living, and many others.

Whatever road you travel towards spiritual growth, Living Flame Press has something to help you on the way, including Robert Wild for charismatic spirituality, John Randall for the seeker in Scripture, René Voillaume for Eucharistic devotion.

We've remembered the children too, with the popular *Noah and the Ark* and others on our expanding list.

Send for our free catalog and see how Living Flame Press can answer your questions.

....

To: Living Flame Press, 325 Rabro Drive, Hauppauge, NY 11788 (Tel. 516 348-5251)

I want to discover Christian answers! Please send me your free catalog.

Name...

Address ....

Town ....Zip ....

SUFFICIENT GRACE
Elfrieda D. Drescher

How God's grace strengthened and sustained a polio victim and her family through more than 25 years of physical, mental and spiritual testing and helped them to find His Kingdom through each other. The inspiring story of one family's journey—with God's help—through years of struggle.

ISBN: 0-914544-66-7 $4.95

FINDING PEACE IN PAIN
The Reflections of a Christian Psychotherapist
Yvonne C. Hebert, M.A., M.F.C.C.

This insightful book offers a positive approach to prayer that will help us to overcome the paralyzing effects of emotional hurt from difficult life situations that can't be avoided or changed. Yvonne Hebert, a practicing psychotherapist, draws from examples involving her own clients in order to show us the way to *Finding Peace in Pain*.

ISBN: 0-914544-53-5 $3.95

DISCERNMENT
Seeking God in Every Situation
Rev. Chris Aridas

The ability to discover God's will and plan for our lives is not only possible but vitally necessary for all who seek to follow the Spirit. Fr. Aridas takes discernment out of the realm of mystery and here sets forth a clear, concise process by which we may find God and thereby discover His will.

ISBN: 0-914544-37-3 $4.95

SOUNDINGS: A Daily Guide Through Scriptural Prayer For Today's Christian
Rev. Chris Aridas

This guidebook for reading Scripture in prayer and meditation is organized around 52 themes, with over 500 scriptural passages and commentary to facilitate personal reflection. A helpful guide for all praying Christians in their journey of faith.

ISBN: 0-914544-71-3 $4.95

COMMUNION OF SAINTS
Rev. George A. Maloney, S.J.

The dynamic love relationship of all the members of the Mystical Body, both living and dead, is a truly consoling and challenging aspect of our faith. The author examines this relationship from historical, psychological, and spiritual standpoints, and discusses its direct effect on our lives.

ISBN: 0-914544-73-X $4.95

SPEAK LORD; I HEAR
Rev. George A. Maloney, S.J.

The author, a renowned spiritual teacher and retreat master, offers us new inspiration as he addresses the universal quest for intimacy with God. The reader is guided to a more focused communion with God through the Holy Spirit.

ISBN: 0-914544-69-1 $4.95